I0187215

BEMBA DYNASTY 2

– A Novel –

CHARLES MWEWA

Copyright © 2024 Charles Mwewa

www.charlesmwewa.com

Published by:

ACP

Ottawa, ON Canada

www.acpress.ca

www.springopus.com

info@acpress.ca

All rights reserved.

ISBN-13: 978-1-988251-75-2

DEDICATION

For

My maternal grandfather,
Chinama Chibwe,

with love.

CONTENTS

PROLOGUE

In a country called Cula or Kola (present day Angola and Congo DR), there was a chief called Mukulumpe "Mierda" *Mubemba*, from whom the *Bemba* people of present-day Zambia derive their name. He had sons by different wives, but one day he heard of a woman with ears as large as an elephant's, who said she came from the sky and belonged to the crocodile (ng'wena) clan. Her name was Mumbi Lyulu Mukasa, and the chief married her. They had three sons, Katongo, Chiti and Nkole, and a daughter, Chilufya Mulenga (Bwalya Chabala II).

The impetuous young men built a tower that fell down and killed people. Mukulumpe was furious. He put out Katongo's eyes, and banished Chiti and Nkole. Mukulumpe pretended to relent and called back the exiles. However, he had dug a game pit to kill the three of them. Katongo, though blind, warned his brothers by using his talking drum. When they arrived at the palace, the king humiliated them by subjecting them do menial work. Chiti and Nkole left the kingdom for good and took with them their three maternal half brothers Kapasa, Chimba and Kazembe, and a maternal cousin, Mwewa, and their entourage.

They fled east, until they came to an area, which at the peak of the kingdom, comprised Lake Tanganyika to the north, Lake Mweru, and Lake Mweru Wantipa to the northwest, Lake Bangweulu and the Luapula River to the west, Lake Nyasa to the east, the Luangwa River to the south, and the Chambeshi River in the middle.

The exiles reached the middle ranges of the Luapula River. Chief Matanda of the Bena Mukulo ferried them across. In their haste, they left behind their blind brother Katongo and their sister Chilufya Mulenga, who Mukulumpe had locked up in a house without doors. They dispatched their half-brother, Kapasa, to free Chilufya Mulenga, which he did ingeniously. But on the way to Luapula, Kapasa fell in love with Chilufya. When it turned out she was pregnant, Kapasa was disowned by Chiti. Meanwhile, the group had fallen in with a 'white magician,' Luchele Ng'anga. When they arrived in Luapula, Kazembe decided to settle there, but Nkole and Chiti were uncertain. When Luchele Ng'anga conjured up a fish from a mortar, they took this to be an omen to head eastwards, and moved toward the plateau of the Chambeshi River, near Lake Bangweulu.

The complexity of their relationships, the reforms that followed, the pain of betrayal in their ranks, their succession disputes, coupled with their tumultuous ritual systems with regards to *Lesa* (God) and *imipashi* (ancestral spirits), and how they traded with the Arabs and braced against the invasion of European traders, explorers, missionaries, and colonist, are the basis of the matters narrated in this trilogy.

A PART OF OUR HISTORY.

CHAPTER 1 | THE MATRIARCH

Queen Matanda's death dealt a deep blow to the emperor. The depth of his sorrow could only be matched by the height of his new responsibility of ensuring that the prematurely born Chiti Chitapankwa, dubbed Chiti III, should grow stronger. Addressing a combined congress of the General Affairs Advisory Council (GAAC) and various committees, the new queen, Queen Bwalya Chabala III, formerly the Lady Chancellor, shocked the congress when she attended the Assembly with the baby prince on her back.

The Assembly reacted with a standing and sustained ovation which lasted for at least thirty minutes. When the applause came to an end, the new queen paid tribute to her predecessor and updated the Assembly on the state of the empire.

"She was a matriarchate, a selfless mother of the empire. She died doing the noble duty that she was ordained to do – giving the empire its next heir," she said this pointing to the baby whom she had just handed over to a wetnurse who was seated beside her.

Again, the entire Assembly stood up for a deafening ovation. And chants of "Bwalya Chabala the Great!" rang loudly across the entire room. The new queen reported that the state of the empire was "strong. The emperor has undergone several misfortunes none of us can endure, and yet, he remains strong and resolute. He will take control of the chamber and empire business once he has finished mourning his beloved Queen Matanda. I will, in the meantime, assume court and palace responsibilities assisted by the two princes."

The speech calmed the Assembly and reassured them of the need for continuity of business.

The new queen continued.

"Having made that salutation and update, today's order of business is…"

The new queen was in the middle of her speech when she heard fidgeting and murmurs in the Assembly.

"May I know what the matter is?" Queen Bwalya Chabala III wanted to know.

"Your Highness, *Chilolo* (counsellor) Mushimba is just baffled that we are getting into business; he thought that today was only…"

"…*playing* politics, no, sir, we are here. It's time to deliberate empire affairs!" The queen interrupted *Chilolo* Kabalika in the middle of his sentence.

Nodding his head, *Chilolo* motioned to the queen to continue.

"Guards, bring him in," ordered the queen.

All in the Assembly were shocked to see Chinyamasako Chikalamo, the emperor's brother, in cuffs.

"Urg, let me go; I'm the true King!" Chinyamasako Chikalamo shouted, exhaling sharply.

The queen locked her lips but kept herself under control so that it was not obvious to the Council members.

"K-e…I mean, keep quiet, you traitor. My dear elders and Council members, this traitor had arranged a coup to unseat his half-brother, your emperor, claiming that the emperor had chosen love over the empire…"

The entire Assembly whooshed. They turned one to another and feasted in a fishbowl of politics for a while in a wild but controlled commotion.

"This *woman* is the real imposter; she is casting aspersions on me because she wants to highjack the rule – see, what she is doing right now…"

"S-t-o-p…stop right there. Guards, bring in the witnesses," the queen, sighing heavily and twitching her left eye, ordered.

Eleven witnesses were brought in who testified against the self-proclaimed King of *Ulubemba.*

Seven more witnesses were summoned in Chinyamasako Chikalamo's defence and they gave evidence for him. But on cross-examination, they all admitted that they were paid to lie, and they asked for forgiveness.

"You heard for yourselves, both from the accused and from our own witnesses. You saw the witnesses breaking right before you. Here is my judgment…"

And just before the queen could pass judgment, there was an interruption, soldiers brought in four people who had been planted at the palace to assassinate the baby prince. When questioned about who ordered the death of the baby prince, the ringleader pointed at Chinyamasako, saying, "He's already installed himself as king, and he paid us to kill the royals."

The Assembly was shocked.

"Here is my judgment. I, Queen Bwalya Chabala III, do sentence you, self-styled *Chitimukulu Bwembya*, who is also known as Chinyamasako Chikalamo, together with all your accomplices, to death by hanging."

The Assembly hailed, "Aye, aye, aye!"

Then the queen gave instructions.

"*Kalikeka*, herald this throughout the empire. This meeting is adjourned!"

CHAPTER 2 | REGENT EXTRAORDINAIRE

The Great Thatched Wall. It swims, climbs, and crawls and sometimes it walks across large expanses of nothing but grassland, jungles, valleys and mountains. It bends its spine into a carnivorous serpentine and coils as it pushes off its leading edge across objects, waters and pounding winds. It stretches out its front body and glides forward by using its belly and rib scales to push backwards. Like a Black Mamba, it has in the last twenty-five years moved swiftly, tacitly at a steady speed of close to twenty kilometers per hour.

It holds and then secretes venom through its delivery system which consists of two venom warrior bases, a compressor military command center, erudite secret agents scattered across the empire, a fang sheath contained in its blind emperor's calculated *ensembles,* timely engendered decrees, and the subtle idea-filled-pouch of its new queen. The combination of its military voluminal and leadership wit, store sufficient quantities of toxins required to effect massive envenomation.

In extent the serpentine, crocodile-shaped empire extended to the Lungu country in the north where it had raided grain farms; Mambweland and Sukumaland in the west where it raided for cattle; Chikwanda in the south where it had initially raided for slaves before the reforms; the Bisa-Kopa country in the southwest where it raided for salt, iron and ivory; Mwamba nation in the center, and Ng'wena and Nkoleland (formerly, Chatindubwi) in the east.

***

It's been over sixteen years since the death of Queen Matanda and the birth of the heir to the throne, the newly crowned prince, Chiti III, and, of course, the ascension to power as Queen Bwalya Chabala III of the *Ulubemba*, of the former Lady Chancellor, Maluba Cheswa Mwewa, who led massive reforms for the reordering and reorganization of the once scattered, nomadic Bemba Kingdom into an earth-shaking dynasty. Her influence and power in the empire were only secondary to that of the emperor, and some observers said that she was the shadow emperor and without her, "the empire is only half."

Queen Bwalya Chabala III herself walked the blind emperor into the Assembly Hall and began the order of business herself on the emperor's behalf. The emperor's brilliance and statesmanship had only accelerated with Queen Bwalya Chabala III on her side.

People said that if one was not aware of events that had taken place in the empire in the last seventeen years, one would think that Chiti III was a biological son of the queen.

She raised him up herself from childhood and he called her "Mother."

When Chiti III was told that the queen was not his biological mother, he replied, "To me, my mother is the first person I saw when my eyes began to distinguish people, and the first person who tendered and nurtured me when I fell ill or when I hurt myself or when I first fell off the back of the horse. My mother is everything, my mother is Queen Bwalya Chabala III."

***

The new Lady Chancellor, Lady Kasuba Kapasa, the emperor's half-sister, like her predecessor before her, the now crowned queen, was daring, fearless and a formidable leader trusted and loved by many people both in the palace and the empire.

Supreme General, General Kalyata, also known as the God of War, had consolidated the military stance of the empire into an impenetrable wall, dubbed the *Great Thatched Wall of the Bemba Dynasty*.

During his long reign as supreme commander, seventy kingdoms, four hundred chiefdoms and numerous rebellions had been subdued.

The *30-70 Theorem* had neither been modified nor relaxed. It had been estimated that under his command, the empire had secured over six hundred secret agents, intel carriers and military ambassadors.

Under him, and with the successful reforms started by the then Lady Chancellor, the military used all tactics and strategies, such as poisons, bees, amphibian warriors (who were swimming tacticians and who masqueraded as a calm lake). No-one crossed the river and entered the empire without their knowledge.

But the greatest threat to the God of War's position had been an emerging star in the empire with skills even General Kalyata himself could not match even when he was younger.

Indeed, General Kalyata as a young man won everyone's praise and adoration when he single-handedly killed a tiger with his own bear hands, earning the title, "Tiger Claws."

However, when a young prince strangled a breastfeeding lioness to death and saved the entire village at Kopa, the empire had revealed a new hero.

And that young prince was no other than Susula Mulenga, the son of Maluba and Emperor Chiti.

Since then, General Susula had risen in rank to be the Deputy Supreme Commander of the empire, second only to General Kalyata in military affairs, and sixth in rank in the entire empire.

Only the emperor, the queen, the crowned prince, General Kalyata, and Lady

Chancellor were above him.

Just when nobody expected for any further reforms, the blind emperor summoned his *Council of Council* as they now called the policy making body comprising the emperor, the former GAAC and all lords, dukes, and ladies.

The *Chilolos* still retained their traditional role of fetching for the king's successor.

A week prior, *Kapaso* Kalikeka, the second-in-command to Mwando, who had now been styled as Chief Counsellor to the Emperor, had met all the *Chilolos* and disclosed to them the emperor's plan.

The emperor had decided to abdicate the throne for his young son to become emperor. The emperor had suggested that he would become regent for the young emperor until the old emperor was satisfied that the young emperor could govern without his father's assistance.

The *Chilolos* had debated for three consecutive days before they came to a unanimous agreement. The only thing they added was that the young emperor should be taught in the intricacies of wisdom and warfare so that, like his father, he should sustain a vast and expansive empire like his father had done.

The suggestion pleased the emperor.

CHAPTER 3 | KASAMA LODGE

“ It's our first wisdom session, Son. Just like Uncle Chimba prepared me for rulership, I am doing the same.”

The new emperor and his father spent a week of nothing but inductive wisdom lectures at Kasama Lodge where they had retreated for that purpose.

The regent's father came to be referred to as Regent Extraordinaire, because of the remarkable manner in which he bequeathed the throne to his young son.

Hon. Sebela had been so impressed with this move that he wrote the following in the royal annals:

> Entry#32134
> Emperor Chiti, today, enters our annals as that giant of faith, of wisdom and of courage, in that order. Of faith, because no matter what the enticement or promise of modern titivations, he never bowed to outside influence. He had been guided by that hallowed

maxim that he had borrowed from the foreigners: *Give to God what is God's and to the king what is the kings.* He took it literally to mean that treat spiritual and traditional things traditionally, and human affairs, humanly.

Wisdom, because, hitherto, no ruler before him has had the wisdom to rule and the understanding of the intimate needs of his people and fulfilling these two equitably without sacrificing one for the other.

And courage, because he is blind – not because he lost his eyes in battle or through a debilitating disease – but because of his love for his people, for God and tradition…

Above all, he understands that empire building, and rulership are eternal missions, and he has the wisdom to know when to pass the button in the quest to establishing a perpetual state…

Then the Regent Extraordinaire began his lectures.

"First, Son, you must be a *successful* ruler, not a *wise* one. If province allows, be both."

The new emperor listened attentively and asked questions where needed and his father took all the time explaining and clarifying points.

The new and young emperor learned that a successful reign won *wars*, though it might lose some *battles*. He also learned that a wise reign was admired but only in so far as the conquest had first been secured, because as the Regent Extraordinaire said, "No matter how wise you are, your people can only respect you if they have their basic needs met first. And we secure their needs through conquest, Son!"

"And what is the second lesson, Father?" Emperor Chiti III asked.

"Talent comes first before blind loyalty."

"Why, Father, I thought that it was important to recognize subjects for their loyalty?"

"You are right, Son, but experience has taught me the opposite. I built your empire on talent and not loyalty alone. When I met your mother, the Queen Dowager, my dearest wife, Maluba, it was not loyalty at the first sight that drew me to her, it was her talent. The same goes for Kalyata and for Sebela and for…"

"The rest of the pioneering reformers, isn't it so, Father?"

"Yes, you're right, Son."

The young emperor learned that loyalty was inherent in royalty.

The royal business was built around the assignment of rewards and punishments. Therefore, subjects as well as officials understood that if they did well, they would be rewarded, but if badly, they would be punished.

"So, do not poke a ripening boil, Son; let it break and spill the pus on its own."

"Point taken, Father, and what is the third?"

"The third one is the most overlooked principle, but I have found out that it could even rank first. *Trust women but control their emotions; respect men but tame their ambitions.*"

"Hmm…huh…I see. You kept my mother, the late Queen Matanda, my current mother, the Queen Dowager, Bwalya Chabala III, Auntie Kasuba and Lady Kapambwe together, and for a long time even when all of them had amatory interest in you?"

"Yes, Son, and more."

"What is it, Father?"

"When we give a sperm to women, we trust that they would carry it to term and bear us children, don't we?"

"Yes, Father."

"Similarly, when you trust a woman with responsibility, they gather everything within them to perform it, as if it was entrusted to them by nature. But their weakness is their emotional spurts, if you can manage that, you are a wise man. But…"

"Women and snakes are alike."

"What do you mean, Father?"

"Every woman, however noble and well intentioned, carries a pouch of venom within them."

"Interesting. Can you elaborate, Father?"

"Sure. When a woman is pressed hard against the wall, they will attack your values and principles – sort of, to force you to 'insult God,' or despise your manliness, as it were."

"I see, thank you, Father. But what about men?"

"Do not work or entrust responsibility to a man you can't respect. No matter how innocuous or small in the eyes of people his task might be, assure him that you find him worthy to do or undertake such responsibility. Men's responsibilities define them, and a small success in it, builds their confidence."

"And what about the second part, that of ambition?"

"Right, with that small or big success comes puffing up with ambition for more, and that is…"

"Why they need to be tamed, I get you, Father."

"But remember, too, that a man is destroyed faster by his success than by his failure!"

"I get it, thank you, Father."

Then the father and his son, the emperor, realized that they had been talking for almost half a day. They did other things and retired to bed.

***

Early the next morning as agreed, they left to hunt.

Emperor Chiti III loved hunting.

He had been so influenced by the foreign embellishments that he had acquired a great deal of foreign insignia and regalia.

For example, he was the first in the empire to acquire a saddle for his horse, which he called *Bwanankulu*, and cowboy boots and a hat from the White Fathers, missionaries, and traders from the East.

He had a knack for gun love and skillset for gun use that he always had three guns on him.

White missionaries called him, "The African Cowboy."

Because of his being too close to foreign culture, the foreign missions celebrated when they learned that he had assumed the reign, although they never said it or showed it openly.

***

That morning, the sun rose up early and smiling. The wind was just perfect for bullets for the son and arrows for the father.

The father was being driven in a chariot, but the son chose to ride on *Bwanankulu*. As they rode side by side, the father first paused, and then started.

"Son, kingdom management is like hunting."

"What do you mean, Father?"

"The hunter must be skilled and work hard just to catch one booty, but a hunted animal must be skilled and know how not only to recognize a predator but to hide from it."

"That seems obvious to me, Father."

"Indeed, but do you see the connection, Son?"

"I think I do. The hunter must work hard and so should the hunted?"

"Partly, Son. What the hunter took home was partly due to the hunter's skill and partly due to the hunted's carelessness. A missed animal can either get depressed and die from fear or it can get smart and devise better ways of avoidance."

"So, Father, how does that liken to kingdom management?"

"Everything. Take *these* foreigners as an example. What do you think they came all the way from their cold lands to these hot terrains, to seek warmth, wealth, or booty?"

"I guess, to spread their Christian message, Father?"

"But why then do they trade?"

"So that they can survive, Father, am I

right?"

"Partly, again, partly, Son."

The Regent Extraordinaire ordered the charioteers to follow a western path that led to the Kasama Vault.

There, what they found baffled the young emperor.

"Bring him out!" The Regent Extraordinaire ordered.

Then *he* was brought out with both legs tied; *his* beard had not been shaved for a long time. At first the young emperor did not recognize *him*. He looked like an animal. He was filthy, stinking, and thin.

"What is *this*, Father?"

"Look. Look very closely."

"O my God. Isn't this one that old priest, F-a-t-h-e-r *Inginato*, Father?"

"You're right. He came like a lamb, but he was a spy for his government or mission abroad. He was bent on destroying my empire to replace it with their Holy Soldiers. Here are all his letters which he sent and received…" The Regent Extraordinaire threw a stash of letters in his son's hands.

"What are these?"

"*Mwango*, read."

After Mwango had read the letters, the young emperor simply sank in his chair, speechless. His eyes kept gazing at the roof. He was in deep thoughts.

"Son, Son!" The Regent Extraordinaire shook his son to awaken him from the temporary stupor.

"I am here, Father. But how did you get all these letters?"

"As I was saying, *the hunter had become the hunted.* It was Maimona, may her soul rest in peace. She had infiltrated this imposter's parish as a nun and provided the empire with the valuable intel for a space of almost ten years, Son."

"You're a genius, Father. So, if Maimona didn't pass away, she would have been providing you with intel still. Oh, wonderful!"

"Yes, Son."

"A…n…d, it's plain here and they didn't even mince words – you were their target all along. They wanted all your wealth and then all your land. Oh, how despicable, how deceiving!" The new emperor stammered.

"Yes, Son. And if she didn't die from natural causes, she would have been my first spy to be planted right at their base in a place they call *Londē*. This deceiver *here* (pointing to Father Ignatius), had even prepared to send Maimona to his country. He was going to be praised for having successfully converted a 'baboon' as he put it in one of his letters to his wife!"

Then Father Ignatius, having heard all the tricks they had set against him and that it was Sister Mary, as he had renamed Maimona, who had outplayed him, got very angry and shrieked rebelliously.

"You and you, you will see. You think that you are smart, wait until our final blow…"

"Shut up, you disgraced priest, don't speak to my father or to me like that, don't you know who we are!"

The Regent Extraordinaire turned softly to his son and whispered in his ears, "Son, lesson number five, *give your enemy chance to say everything they have in their mind. In anger, they can reveal so much truth. They will unveil plans, stratagems and all the evil they are going to do!*"

"I understand, Father."

So, from then, the young emperor never disturbed Father Ignatius as he ranted and seethed. From his rage and rancorous speech, they learned that the *foreigners* were using a close relative of the emperor to overthrow the young ruler. Although the disgraced priest did not say his name, both the emperor and his father suspected someone they knew but they could not say it to one another.

"'Take him away for now!" The Regent Extraordinaire ordered.

When the disgraced priest had gone, the young emperor turned quickly to his father; he had several concerns.

"Father, it was reported…"

"'That he had been mowed by wild animals and his bloody clothes were shipped to *Londē*,' that's right. It is just one of those tricks we also have learned to play, Son."

"What if they find out that it was not his blood, Father?"

"We took care of that. We used the blood of another *foreigner* who had succumbed to malaria."

"But how did you catch him seeing that he was always surrounded by men with *ngwanis*?"

"It is called 'The Replacement,' General

Kalyata's men will brief you on that. So, we paired exactly the same number of his entourage, same height, same shape, and same looks. When they took their rest, our pairs went in, killed everyone, and replaced them with themselves. This imposter couldn't recognize the difference when he woke up the next morning. They even had the opportunity to see whom he was meeting and plotting with, Rev. *Emenshindele* (Emmasdale) at Mindolo Homestead in Mambweland."

"What happened to Rev. *Emenshindele*, did you also catch him, Father?"

"No, Son. You need a large bait to catch a big fish. His time will come. Right now, we have spies around him gathering verifiable intel."

"I surely have a long way to learn from you, Dad."

"Indeed, you have. But you are like me, you will learn quickly."

The two, a father and his son, grew even more attached, shared a laugh and then Regent Extraordinaire ordered that they should bring to him "the foreigner's *lutuku* (whiskey)."

When the young emperor tried it, he

quickly swashed it off his mouth.

"It's too strong, this is *kachasu*, isn't it?"

"Yes, but we didn't brew it; they did," The Regent Extraordinaire pointed in the direction where they were holding Father Ignatius.

"This is another lie, Son. They preach in their mission stations that it is sin to drink alcohol, but privately and secretly they imbibe recklessly something even stronger than *katata* or *katubi*."

"Sort of, their alcohol is holy but ours is dirty?"

"Some sort of that, Son."

They spent a night in the manse at the Kasama Volt, and when saying goodnight to his son, the emperor, the father also said, "Sleep tight, Son, tomorrow we are in for a big hunt."

***

Early the next morning, they were awakened to a craw's sound, "Caw-caw-caw-caw koodle-yah!"

Outside it was dark and dewy.

The servants had already been awakened preparing for the two to go out for the hunt.

"Son, it's time to go. And just before I forget, I want you to understand that you're one step ahead if you're attacked by an enemy who fights properly, with rules. Such are predictable, and easily defeatable. But not *these*, they don't fight with rules, but with intrigue, secrets. Never forget that."

"Over my dead body, Dad."

The servants led the way towards a dense forest and after they had passed a stream and climbed a small hill, there *he* was.

"What? Father, this is…"

"Yes, Son, this is your very first hunt. You must shoot and kill!"

He stood in between two poles, and both of his hands and legs were tied to the four corners of the poles. A dark cloth covered his face. He was saying something, but it was inaudible. He was going to be killed with the same guns that he supplied. The emperor hesitated, and he was sweating profusely.

"Father, if this is what you will, I will do it?" The emperor inquired.

"There is no other way, Son," the father

assured his son.

"But, Dad, I have never done anything like this…but…but what about his trial…doesn't he have rights to even say…"

"I know, Son. First shoot him, and then we shall discuss the rest."

The young, naive emperor took aim, and a sound was heard, "Kaboom!"

***

The emperor could not ride his own horse, *Bwanankulu*, but rather, he sandwiched himself in his father's carriage between his father and Mwando, who had accompanied them.

He was shivering and exasperated. But neither his father nor Mwando paid any particular attention to him. To them, it was like business as usual.

They traveled for about three kilometers without saying a word.

Light drizzles swathed the land momentarily and then disappeared.

And a late awakening rooster faintly crowed in the far distance, "Cock-a-doodle-doo!"

"But, Father," began the young emperor, "Why didn't you show him mercy?"

"This is lesson number…"

"Six, Your Majesty," stimulated Mwando.

"Yes, six it is. Mercy and wrath are the two sides of the same coin, Son. You can only expense one at a time. Expensing one rather than the other at the wrong time, and failure to expense one rather than the other at the right time, are injurious to both divine and moral imperatives. You must be decisive and be willing to expense the appropriate response, mercy, or wrath, when they are demanded, all the time. Don't hesitate."

"What about a *trial*, Father, don't you think he deserved to tell his side of the story?"

"You're right. Everyone deserves a right to be heard, Son, even criminals. But remember that a trial dignifies the process, not the outcome. A man may be found guilty or be acquitted, and all that eventually doesn't matter to the people. What satisfies them is the understanding that the process was fair. But there is one exception, for a person who is caught in a treasonous act, trial is implied, Son."

"Why, Father?"

"Because a man or woman who commits treason or who is a traitor or betrayer, violates the ultimate guarantee of mercy, trust. Punishment for such must be swift and without hesitation, Son."

"But God…"

"Stop right there, Son. It's an imperative for God and gods to exercise mercy when it befits them. It's imperative for kings and emperors to impose mercy only when trust is possible later. Even their God would dare not forgive Satan because God cannot trust him."

Mwando parted the young emperor on his left shoulder, and whispered, "*Take that nugget without a pint, Your Majesty.*"

***

The young emperor pondered at length on all that he had learned from his father, and concluded, *No wonder he managed to build such a great empire, Father is a thinker!*

And as they neared Kasama Lodge, the emperor turned to his father and asked, "Is there anything more I should know?"

"Yes, Son. Don't entrust your throne to another *man* who can potentially replace you, even if it's just for a moment. When you are absent, bestow responsibility on a trusted *woman*. As I said earlier, a woman takes better care of those things which are entrusted to her. Always have a woman you can trust and entrust your royal responsibility to when you are not there."

"But…did I make a mistake, Father, why didn't you correct me?"

"Yes, you did, but I wanted you to learn a lesson first. Yes, he's your brother, but Susula can potentially replace you, therefore, he qualifies to be among those you can't entrust your throne to in your absence."

That last point, not only did it unsettle the emperor, but it brought him great apprehension, having connected it to what the shamed priest he just shot said.

"Can we return to Ng'wena, Father?"

"Yes, now, you are ready to rule, Son."

CHAPTER 4 | NG'WENA SPEECH

At Ng'wena, it wasn't life as usual. By noon day, the shadow must have been running late. It had an unusually longer angle than the usual short one. It was as if the sun was weeping. But what had remained the same was the fact that the crowd had shown up like always when it had been summoned.

At first, it was one or two people who showed up around what was called the *Insaaka* or the platform. Then it began to grow bigger and bigger until all that could be heard was the buzzing of many sounds.

The emperor took the stand on the stage. He raised and clenched his right fist.

"Silence. Silence!"

"The emperor wants to speak!"

"Let him talk."

"What's going on?"

People were shouting and asking similar questions, but it was clear that the emperor had something important to say. Soon as there was silence, the emperor began to speak.

"In fact, today, it's my father who will speak on my behalf. Dad, please come and address *our* people."

The blind, graceful Regent Extraordinaire stood up with the aid of his personal assistant, Mwando, and after waving to the crowd, he cleared his throat and took the stand.

> Friends and natives,
> We silenced a once holy man of God today.
> In our custom, with no trial we don't slay
> But claims against him were probative.
> Sisters and brothers,
> We don't forgive *this* wrong, betrayal,
> Even if the culprit happens to be royal.
> Indeed, truth, every crime it smothers.
> Fellow inhabitants,
> We are only as strong as our gift of land;
> Many forces wouldn't want us to expand
> For they are nothing but contaminants.
> Dearly esteemed compatriots,
> We have reports of raids in the outskirts
> We know these are not isolated outbursts
> Since these rioting chiefs are patriots.

My loved ones,
When we give an inch to the colonizers
They'll deem themselves modernizers;
They'll erase our past, rewrite their
owns.
Beloveds,
Already, they question our intellect,
They intend to reduce us to a mere sect,
Becoming insipid recipients of aids.
Families of *Ulubemba*,
Colonizers will steal our history,
Replacing our folklore with their story,
Beware, watch, children of Mubemba.
My lads,
Even now, they pit us against each
other,
They divide sister against brother
Breaking moms against dads.
My dearest,
They will corrupt our environment
To beggars, reducing us to our
detriment
On our own soil, making us mere
guests.
My cherished people,
If they find weak leadership someday,
They will manipulate it in some way
Breaking asunder our legacy's steeple.
Listen, beloved of our ancestors,
It will be too late for their trimmings,
They consider our land their winnings
They'll charge us rent for our shelters.
People of my tribe,

If we cede, we won't only lose our land,
But our identity, our *names*, our garland
Then our *language*, all for a paltry bribe.
My worthy subjects,
Culture, language, identity are our trinity
When taken away, we lose our nobility
Making it difficult to reconstruct.
Offspring of Bwalya Chabala,
They'll subject you to foreign education
Forcing you into self-doubt as a nation,
Teaching British stories in your
Shambala.
I submit to you all,
That today they consider us comrades,
But in future they'll treat us as farm
lads;
They'll deculturate us, leading to a fall.
My people, my kind,
I may not be there with you in that time,
But remember these words of who I'm,
I can clearly see the future though blind.

As the Regent Extraordinaire ended his speech, some people were crying, saying, "We have never been ruled by someone as wise as you."

Others were worried not knowing how his young son would handle some complex future issues of foreign intrusion.

"God protect us," one woman, wearing only a *chitenge* wrapper around her waist, leaving her breasts wondering in the sand of bare-stamping feet, prayed.

But when the emperor and his father held hands and began to wave to the crowd, the audience erupted into a prolonged chant as the two royals were being escorted away by the warrior guards.

Long live Chiti II!
Long live Chiti III!
Long live Bembaland!
Long live the empire!

The son led his blind father along until they reached the carriage. Before he stepped into his seat, the blind father squeezed his son's right hand tightly, as he had done to him as a child.

"Son, I have done everything for you to be a great leader."

"Yes, Dad, I know. But I am afraid, your speech…"

"My speech, Son, is both your guide and a warning. Remember the proverb, *Uluse lwalile inkwale* (mercy feasted on a partridge)."

There was a moment of silence as the son tucked his father securely into the seat.

The son was just about to turn and go to his own seat when his father searched for his hand, found it and again squeezed it, this time a little bit tighter.

"I have studied *them*, *their* behavior, Son. There is a presumption of superiority among their rank. This will make it easier for them to conquer us. Our people have a weakness, they trust too quickly before they verify."

"I hear you, Fa…" Chiti III wanted to continue.

"…and they will demand perfection from us, which they, themselves aren't able to achieve. They will do all this because of …" Chiti II was also stopped in midsentence.

"…*ngwanis*, Father, I know."

"Hmh…" Chiti II hummed.

The carriage took off via a smoothly paved path leading to the palace.

Father and son uttered no words.

They both seemed to be fixated on the windows, watching as trees retreated backwards as the caravan raced forward.

The grass was still green, and the sky still blue.

***

At the Chief Records Office, astride the Chanda Munungu Hall, the Chief Records Officer, Lord Sebela, summoned his first assistant, Officer Makwerere, to receive important instructions.

"*Makwerere*, add this to the records."

"Yes, sir. I am ready to write down."

"Write:

> In the prime years of Bembaland when our mother, Chilufya Mulenga, honored the realm by leading the delegation under the military command of Hon. Lord Chimba to Kapelembe, there the institution of the first regal royal of the Miti Clan was inaugurated. In what came to be called the 'Great Kapelembe Speech,' the young king won the hearts and souls of his people, including the reunification of the *Ingulo Troupe* into mainstream Bemba structure. He ruled with uncontaminated wisdom and wholesome integrity until he abdicated the reign for his dear son, Emperor Chiti III. His was a rule blessed by the gods and envied by the mortals. But his real genius had not been revealed until he left a vivid script of the intrusions

about the *foreigners* who had begun to infiltrate the realm in order to rid it of its traditions and customs.

He was strong and determined to safeguard his son's reign by educating him in the intricacies of statehood and common affairs. The former emperor, then styled as Regent Extraordinaire, schooled his son strongly on the signs and methods those who traveled from far lands would unleash in order to subject his people to colonialism and servitude. However, his greatest speech had not been heard until today, the first year of his son's reign in the month when kings go for royal retreats.

Let it be known to the whole of Bembaland, that in his greatest speech ever, which we now dub, *'The Ng'wena Speech,"* His Excellency, Majesty Exceptionnaire, Royal Emeritus, king of kings, the Regent Extraordinaire, Chiti Chilufya Chileshe Chepela, Chiti the Second, did warn of turbulent times when the empire would be imperiled by distress and colonialism. In those days, the former emperor warned, *foreigners* would grab *these* lands, change *our* names and language, and replace them with their own.

Beware and be watchful.

Ends the record Entry#4587982."

His left hand still dripping with black ash ink, Makwerere stretched himself to the point of almost dropping the ash brush to the ground. He hesitated, and then asked for clarification.

"S-sir, should I add your initials to this report?"

It was more of a rhetorical question than a direct inquiry. Throughout his career, beginning when he was conscripted into the royal records department as a young man, to when his department was inundated with the transcription of the voluminous legal documentations arising from the historical Maluba Reforms, he had never known his boss to endorse records without his name.

As for the Chief Records Officer, he sounded more like someone who had just run a one hundred meters sprint than a five thousand five hundred meters marathon. And without any hesitations he responded.

"No, Makwerere. This is what is on the mind of everyone who listened to the royals today. I simply put in words their thinking and feelings."

"Alright, sir, it is done."

CHAPTER 5 | DEADLY TRIANGLE

A gentle breeze of the Bangueulu plains oozed calmly on the surface of his battle-hardened skin. At his cottage overlooking the confluence where the Chambeshi River met the great wetland of his time, General Kalyata stood astride a *mwembe tree* drinking his local brew of *katata*.

On guard, in a fading view from the camp, were about fifty warrior guards carrying shields of rattan and wood with metallic heads. They were also carrying bows and arrows. And surrounding his hut, were about seven special elite warriors each carrying a gun and a *bakuba* spear.

Inside his hut, lying naked on his bamboo-crafted bed with a mattress filled with bastard camphor tree leaves to repel mosquitoes and other pests, was a familiar face and name in the empire.

"Darling, please come in, I am *dying* to die here?" Lady Kapambwe dared the God of War.

"You make it feel light, Darling, but I have not slept a second since the young man confronted me," General Kalyata said.

"But it's not you the old emperor will kill if this goes public. It is me. I am the one who lied that I was impregnated by him."

"It's not just a matter of attributing blame, Love, it's more a matter of trust. There is nothing in this empire that either the old emperor or his successor son has denied me. That thought alone is killing me."

"Come on, you're turning me off," Lady Kapambwe held the General from the back while in her natural-born uniform, and before long the two were in bed jostling and wrestling each other in a romantic bout.

But the romantic getaway was short-lived. After midnight, General Kalyata was already up.

"Wake up, Kapambwe, wake up."

The General addressed his lover by her first name.

"W-what…I…thought we had talked, Darling," Lady Kapambwe squirmed as her eyelids quirked disbelievingly.

"General Susula is coming in six hours' time, and we need a plan. We need to know what to say and how to respond."

"But you know already what he wants?"

"I do. But I am afraid. For the first time in my life, I fear not so much for my life as for the sense of betrayal I will bring to the royals. I don't know why I agreed to meet the young man."

"Don't dwell on it, Darling. Susula can kill the *boy*. Period. After that, he's on his own."

"But you don't still get it, do you?" General Kalyata squawked, the only time in their over-thirty-year secret affair he had ever lost his temper against her.

Lady Kapambwe was visibly shaken.

General Kalyata realized that he had upset her by hurting her feelings, and he apologized.

"Sorry, Love. As you can see I…I am roasted here."

They sat there quietly for almost two hours, each doing their own thinking. General Kalyata stood up and began to pace the floor end to end. Lady Kapambwe cramped herself up in the corner of the room in silence, she was almost breathless.

A beam of sunlight entered the room through tiny crevices in the clay-painted hut. And then both lovers talked almost at the same time:

"Dress up..."
"Do you trust them…?" Lady Kapambwe asked.

***

Lady Kapambwe heard, and she began to dress up. But the General missed the lover's question.

"What did you say?" General Kalyata asked his lover to repeat herself.

"I was wondering if your guards would not tell on you when the young man comes."

The now fully dressed lover stretched herself and stressed her point.

"They are disciplined. Even so, they know that he's coming here to moot on security logistics concerning the upcoming *Ukusefya Pang'wena* cerebrations."

The atmosphere was tense.

General Kalyata had considered many options, the least of which was to kill

General Susula *right here and throw his body in the lake*, he had thought.

But what if he comes prepared, which I think is what he will do, the General continued to think.

Lady Kapambwe remembered that sad, fateful day when Susula overheard her conversation with her son, Nkole II. Nkole II and Susula were then sharing a cottage assisting their father with palace governance affairs because the senior emperor was attending to his ailing wife, the late Queen Matanda. Nkole II was worried that her mother had made him live a lie all his life, "…because of that greed of yours. My father is General Kalyata, but you have made me call a total stranger, the emperor, my father. I don't care if he is a god of the world itself."

Lady Kapambwe had then comforted her son and then warned, "It's for you and your father's sake that I did what I did. You will be king someday and then you could reveal yourself to the empire. For now, it is better to keep it this way."

Susula was listening to the conversation, but the duo did not know. They thought that Susula had left the cottage, but he had been delayed due to a flu-like symptom he had had that afternoon. He was quietly listening, except for when Lady Kapambwe had mentioned Nkole II to become the next emperor. Before that, Susula had no vested interest in their conversation. He did not want them to know that he was, in fact, eavesdropping on them.

But when Nkole II had asked his mother how he could become king ahead of Susula who was older than him, Lady Kapambwe had answered, "Leave that to me; I will make him *disappear.*"

"What do you mean by 'disappear'?" Nkole had asked his mother for clarification.

And what she said next, upset Nkole II and exposed Susula's position.

"I will *kill* him. That's what I will do. Your father will help me do that!"

When Susula heard those words, he choked and stumbled, as Nkole II shouted in astonishment, "No, *he* is the only brother I have ever known. You can't kill him."

Then there was some noise.

Someone had wheezed or was choking.

"Ssh! I heard a cough; you told me that

there was no-one present other than you."

Before Nkole II could respond, Susula had emerged from the shadows and he spoke out, "Stop right there. I heard everything. It's too late!"

***

Coming back to the cottage, Lady Kapambwe was in agony. As she pondered on those events, her visage turned pale, and she cramped herself even tighter into the corner.

She also remembered how she had pacified or how Susula had solved the potential problem. When Lady Kapambwe had pleaded with him not to disclose what he had heard, Susula had come up with a plan.

"I am not going to tell anyone what you said," Susula had offered.

"Really, but how do I trust you?" Lady Kapambwe had inquired.

"Under one condition. That Nkole II ceases to desire the throne and that you and General Kalyata support me in taking over my father's throne."

It was a hard bargain but both Nkole II

and Lady Kapambwe had consented.

Now years had passed and a true heir to the throne had been born. All that General Susula now wanted was to deal with a double blow, kill the new and young emperor and exile his own blind father.

***

"Generals, I summoned you here because of a breach on our southern frontier. I am sure you already know," Emperor Chiti II said while caressing the inner thighs of the newest member of the Harlem, an Aushi concubine seconded by the queen.

"Majesty, *amenshi yakutali tayashimya mulilo* (literally, from afar, water cannot extinguish a local fire)," General Kalyata assured the emperor.

"And you need not worry, Father, we are not called *Aba*Bemba for nothing, our name means a great land – as expansive as a sea; we shall drown these Ngoni warriors who are only good for butchering pregnant mice!"

The two generals, the Supreme Commander and his deputy provided their battle strategy and how they would *drown* the Ngoni warriors on the southern border of the empire.

They debriefed their commander-in-chief that they had set up nine companies and one troupe under their command.

General Kalyata commanded the companies stationed at Isandulula near Lake Mweru, at Keleka near Lake Bangweulu, at Chulung'oma, and at Kashi-ka-Lwena.

Those would provide support to the companies led by General Susula which guarded the frontier border under the embankments of the Safwa Rapids astride the Chambeshi River, and the rest of his companies had set up defenses near Mulambalala, Chitabata, Chibambo, and at Ipunga.

The designated vanguard under a young cadet, a promising and up-and-coming, general-to-be, Prince Mporokoso Totilo, son of Ndalasha Totilo who the first chief was to be appointed from a non-royal line in *Lubemba*, would command a troupe of investigative agents at Chikilu, and those had been collecting intel and reporting directly to General Kalyata.

Staring his blind father directly in the face, the young emperor gave a vote of confidence in an audaciously led command under generals Kalyata and Susula.

"We go steady and riled under the guiding warrior *imipashi* (spirits) of Mwene Kongo Mvemba, *Mubemba* himself, our original Nzinga ur-ancestor – warrior of warriors, and under the *imipashi* of our ancestral grandmothers, Bwalya Chabala and Mumbi Lyulu Mukasa, progenitors of us all, the *Bena-Ng'andu-Bena-Ng'wena* clan. We shall expel these vagabonds, Father. We shall prevail!"

The assurances and declarations from the two generals pleased the emperor who blessed them and sent them away on the perilous mission.

CHAPTER 6 | BLACKMAIL

"I came prepared, General. Fortunately, you kept your word. None of my men was hurt. But forgive me, I have had all your men bound up, just as a precaution. Let us get straight to business."

"That was not necessary, General Susula," General Kalyata advised politely.

General Susula had, indeed, taken all precautions before boarding for the island where they were scheduled to meet, him, General Kalyata and Lady Kapambwe.

General Susula had sent spies disguised as fishers and they had been monitoring all the movements on the island. The only thing they reported to Susula was that "The light in General Kalyata's hut did not go off the entire night."

A former serviceman who had served under General Kalyata's regiment before, comforted General Susula when he noted that, "It's the General's MO or method of operation; he's never seen to stop working even at night."

Regardless, General Susula had come with over two hundred men who had surrounded the island ready to fight. He had over sixty more men than General Kalyata had.

At the meeting with the two lovers, General Susula refused to accept water or alcoholic beverages, nor did he take a seat. Both Generals knew very well that a poisoned drink or seat was the first rule of friendly warfare.

A news bearer had already reported to General Kalyata that General Susula's men had outnumbered his own men and that each of the more than one hundred and forty warriors he saw, had a gun.

One hundred and forty warriors bearing ngwanis, *where did this boy acquire so many* ngwanis? *We have only six hundred guns in the entire empire, and they are all locked under strict protocol and only I can authorize their release. So, where did he get them?* General Kalyata pondered.

"I keep my words, General Susula."

"You better, General. Your own reputation is staked on it."

"And how is this going to work,

General Susula?" Lady Kapambwe asked.

Then General Susula went into an elaborate plan already put in place. There were over one thousand armed men already positioned. Two hundred were with him on the island. Six hundred would infiltrate the celebration. One hundred and fifty would impale the palace guards, paving the way for General Susula to occupy a vacant throne, as fifty warriors armed to the teeth were on a suicide mission to assassinate the young emperor while he performed his "first and last *Ukusefya Pang'wena*," as General Susula put it.

General Kalyata and Lady Kapambwe also learned that one hundred and fifty chiefs, ninety-six kings and three Christian missions out of the eight in the land had aligned with General Susula.

So, it was the missions that gave him the ngwanis, General Kalyata contemplated.

"And what is the role of my son, Nkole II, and his kingdom in all this?" Lady Kapambwe wanted to know.

"King Nkole II will be with me at all times…"

"What do you mean by he will be 'with

me at all times'? I hope you didn't kidnap him?" Lady Kapambwe said, sniveling.

"Don't worry, Mother, I did it as a precaution. Soon as I confirm the death of that imposter, I will gladly release him to you, safely."

There was a pause, and only Lady Kapambwe's sobs trended intermittently.

General Kalyata, as his pattern of behavior had been, was a man of few words. Most of his talking was done in his mind.

So, he kidnapped the lad to force me and Lady Kapambwe to oblige. That way he knows he has leverage in case of any mishap, brilliant tactician, very ambitious kid, General Kalyata analyzed.

"As for you, God of War," turning towards General Kalyata, "You will command the elite forces to stay put or create a diversion until the exercise is completed. If…"

"I hear you, there is no need. I will have the order one hour before the match. I just want one guarantee…"

"And what is it?"

"No-one lays a finger on the *person* of the Regent Extraordinaire, your father!"

"That was settled in our initial meeting,

General, remember?"

"I do. I just want to make sure."

General here loves the old man, one would think I was his servant, and the General was his son, but what can I do, the renegade sealed his fate when he relegated me to be his infant's dog, General Susula considered.

"As for you, Mother…"

"What about me?"

"I have decided that you are not leaving this place for a while…?"

"What? You are kidnapping me, too?"

"I won't call it a *kidnap*, regard it as an extended vacation. You will join us at our celebrations later. By the way, I intend for you to be the Queen Dowager when the dust is settled."

"What about Maluba, what will you do to your *own* mother?"

"She…" General Susula grinded his teeth, "She hurt me more than anyone in this whole world…I hate her…I hate her so much. First, she prefers another woman's child to her own son. Second, I…I am very much sure of this, she was the one who gave that imposter of a father the useless idea of installing another woman's baby as emperor instead of me.

She will get her desserts!"

General Kalyata did not talk much during the entire time, about four hours of planning, not really planning, of General Susula explaining his already planned coup to the two.

"I am sure you will easily succeed," General Kalyata began, "…but I have two questions, not two really, one is an observation."

"Hmm…I…I am listening," General Susula prompted.

"What would you do with me, and shouldn't you be investing in beginning well, instead of being vindictive?"

General Susula parted the God of War lightly on the back, "*Father*, you are like a father I never had. You will be my military counsellor, after all, you are the God of War."

"And on my observation?"

"Aren't you the one who taught me that one can't win a war if they are thinking of dying? Aren't you also the one who wrote the manual of warfare. On line 103 you said, 'If any emotion is coveted during war, it should be anger, because it is short and lethal,' am I not correct, General?"

"That is war…"

"But *this* is also war to me, don't you get it, General!"

General Susula got really furious, but he then quickly relented, "Sorry, General, I blew it, but don't worry, I will learn to control my anger as emperor."

"One last request, General Susula?"

"Say it, General."

"Give the emperor a dignified burial at Milemba so that he can rest with his ancestors."

"I will think about it. This meeting is over here. Talk is cheap, it's now time to act. *Kamfwa*, take my mother here to her hut. Assign thirty strong and skilled warriors to guard her until you receive instructions from me. If she runs away or dies, kill yourself and your regiment before I come, you hear me?"

"Yes, Commander!" Shouted Colonel Kamfwa Yamfwa.

"God of War, let us go," General Susula ordered.

***

"May I come in, Mother?"

"You may, Son. I have been waiting for you."

"What is it that's so urgent, Mother, that you called for me?"

It was the season when the mangos ripened in Bembaland. Almost every child on the dusty street was eating one. During this period, the world looked much like an orangery – green, orange, and warm – perfect for camouflage, too. It was also the season when every household was preparing itself to take part or to watch the most important ceremony of the year, *Ukusefya Pang'wena*.

And that year was special because the young emperor would be leading the procession. The old emperor, the Regent Extraordinaire, would be seated at Mungwi where he would welcome the imperial retinue when it completed the stately voyage.

"Nothing is so urgent, Son. The emperor wanted me to relay a message that you should go to Mambweland and give Rev. Baxter this invitation to attend *Ukusefya Pang'wena*."

The Queen Dowager handed to her son a small plaque.

The matriarch then concentrated on feeding the homing pigeons as she sang to them the same lullaby she used to sing when Susula was a baby.

General Susula took a seat, and he did not seem busy anymore.

"Do you remember when I began training these?" The matriarch pointed to the birds she was feeding.

"Of course, they were six weeks old, five years ago."

"Remember when I placed them in loft, and confined them for seven days, you remember what you told me, Son?"

"Of course, I do. I can say the same today."

"Say it?" The mother dared her son.

""The element of routine is a predicator of human consequences. One can get anything if they study their opponents' routines.' That's what I said, and I stand by it today."

"Since then, these birds have followed routines, Son. They know that this is their house, and they can go anywhere but they will always come back. That's what I like about these birds' routines, Son. They always come back."

"So?"

"They internalize time, day, and place. I have conditioned them to associate feeding time with returning to this loft. That's all I can do, but the use to which someone puts their newly acquired skill is anyone's guess."

"*Mother*, why do you always speak in parables? I am old now, talk to me like woman to man!"

"Of course, you are now a man, but to me…"

"Yes, I will always be your baby boy," General Susula completed his mother's sentence.

"Pay attention to details, Son, details, and don't not be sober."

'Don't not be sober,' is what she always told me when I wanted to release the pigeons before they were ready to fly away. And this message of invitation, why today? Why not send the regular Kapaso *to deliver the news? I know, it's because it's this sulking emperor's time to officiate the ceremony and I am sure they want the invitation to strike a code of seriousness. Talking of slaying two birds with one stone,* General Susula thought.

"Bye, Son, don't be late, and *don't….*"

"Of course, Mother '…*not be sober*!'"

CHAPTER 7 | SUSULA REVOLTS

The Crocodile Empire. On the surface and in cold weather, it is calm, naïve, and because it doesn't always attack, it can even be accused of being a riskless, innocuous empire.

However, under the water, it is a menace, and one hundred times deadlier. It can bite, and sometimes, three and a half times more potent than a lion.

It rarely goes hunting, but when it does, it hunts to kill. When the water warms up, round about September to December, it begins to get excited, and with this excitement comes its activism and the knack for hunting.

Among the smartest hunters, it ranks near the top. It lies in wait, studying its would-be victim for days and even weeks – scouting for all its routines and vulnerabilities. And then when the victim least expects, such as when they stand in shallow water or on shores, drinking water or washing clothes, or retrieving fishing equipment, then the empire ambushes with the rate of speed unexpected for the realm of its size.

When it attacks, it aims at holding its prey very tight, with its sharp teeth. Then, it rolls its victim, pulling it underwater, vigorously shaking it, dragging it underwater to drown it.

And whoever it drowns must have been in the wrong place at the wrong time.

***

To: Rev. Baxter, Holy Vicar
From: Bwalya Chabala III, Q.D.

Greetings:

Your Holiness, by the time you receive this letter, either General Susula has already read it and understands its import, or it is too late and the process towards his destruction and that of your vicarship have been put in motion.

His Majesty received intel that my

son has been plotting to overthrow a legitimately installed reign of his young brother, Emperor Chiti III, using *ngwanis* (*imfuti*, as they are now calling them in Kasama) and other support obtained from priests and leaders serving under your vicarship.

It might interest you to know that his father, Regent Extraordinaire, former emperor, Chiti II, my husband, was involved in the disappearance of the Right Bishop, Father Ignatius Paul. Father Ignatius was an associate of yours who before his demise had devoured incriminating information that implicated yourself and those close to you.

We have evidence that you have been aiding and abating my son, General Susula, to use the occasion of *Ukusefya Pang'wena* to assassinate the rightful regal and to capture and exile myself and the Regent Extraordinaire, Chiti II.

As a mother of a nation and a mother to a son, I have been torn in between the interests of one and those of many. And I hope you appreciate that I cannot neglect the health of many to serve the wealth of one rogue child. I have given General Susula enough signs and indications that his efforts are known to us and that if he continues with his attempted coup, he will be met with the lethal teeth of a crocodile.

May I kindly remind you, Your Holiness, that General Susula's fall will not be in seclusion. You and those who have aided and abated him may perish with him. If you assist to stop him, perhaps there is a chance that I may intercede to the realm to forgive you and preserve the mission.

I remain.
Q.D

***

When Rev. Baxter read the letter, he could not hold it together and he fainted. General Susula was in a hurry, and he left immediately, he delivered the letter and got more guns. So, when Rev. Baxter recuperated and wanted his people to stop the General, it was too late; he had already gone.

"Servants, follow the direction General Susula took and bring him back. Tell him that it is a matter of life and death," Rev. Baxter instructed three of his servants.

When the three left on the reverend's own horses to warn General Susula so that he did not proceed with his plot, His Holiness summoned his leadership committee and broke the bad news.

"Brothers, we have landed into hellish waters. Our plan to overcome evil and the works of Satan in this land, has been met with an impediment. General Susula brought to me *this* letter," His Holiness handed over the impugned letter to his leadership team to read.

After they had all read, the place became cold and quiet, as quiet as a cemetery.

"What shall we do, brothers?" Rev. Eugene, the Deputy Vicar asked.

"But how did the plan leak?" Brother Emmanuel Dennison wanted to know.

"You can read it all, it's all in that letter, brothers. Somehow, I knew that that impatient bibber, Ignatius, couldn't be trusted. If him who was very close to the emperor was killed, our days, brothers may be numbered unless the servants find Susula or the Lord intervenes," Rev. Baxter warned.

As they were deliberating, the servants returned.

"Permission to come in, Your Holiness?"

"Please enter, we have been waiting for you."

"Y…Your Highness…"

"Just say it; all of us here are brothers."

"We looked everywhere and asked in every village, he was gone."

That report darkened the atmosphere even further. The middle of the day felt like the darkest of the night to everyone present. Options were now running low. If Susula attacked, he would be walking directly in the trap, and if he was tried, he would reveal who gave him the guns.

"He must have been tortured for him to reveal that we gave guns to the heathens. I mean, Ignatius," remarked Brother Ernesto.

"Of course, this is to be expected of *these* unholy, sinful and uncircumcised Philistines," responded Brother Tyler.

"How many guns do we currently have?" Brother Moses asked.

"About seventy-five in inventory," Rev. Eugene unveiled.

"But what is that for?" Rev. Baxter inquired.

"To kill the heathens, Sir, and establish the Kingdom of God in these godforsaken lands. We have a sizable army and if we can team up with our brother, Chief Nsokolo II, we could bring this regime down," Brother Moses was confident.

"We need to be wise as serpents but calm as doves, brothers. We are outnumbered and Chiti's rule has grown very powerful in the last seventeen years. He has spies in every place, he controls every chief and king almost at will, and even if we were to request reinforcements from overseas, we would all be dead before help came. Like our Lord said, it is better that one should perish than the majority should die…"

"What do you mean, Your Holiness? Remember also that if you strike a shepherd, the sheep will scatter?"

Brother Emmanuel censured the reverend for suggesting that he should give himself over to be killed thereby saving the work of the mission.

The debate continued throughout the night.

***

The rebels had parted into three groups. One group headed by General Milambo Besa went straight to the base of Kalungu River where the emperor was slated to begin the voyage towards Mungwi.

The second group under General Chintu Chabala headed towards Mungwi to abduct the Regent Extraordinaire and the Queen Dowager.

And the last group led by General Susula himself went straight to the palace at Ng'wena to assume the throne.

General Besa's group did not face any resistance at all. When it arrived, one of the warriors immediately entered the tent where the emperor was supposed to be rested and what happened inside there was everyone's guess.

"You came to kill me, I know. I am ready, go ahead. But before you do so, I want you to tell General Susula that I am willing to die for my emperor, though I am not him," a person who looked exactly like Emperor Chiti III explained.

That was the first sign that not all was well. General Besa was disoriented. He squeezed his eyes shut and then he silently gave himself a second opinion, *I am just imagining things. This is, indeed, the emperor.*

He paced the floor several times, and then initiated a tête-à-tête with the person masquerading as Emperor Chiti III.

"I know you are Emperor Chiti III, right?"

"I am."

"You know I am here to kill you, right?"

"I know. But before you do so, take a look outside."

When General Besa looked outside

he could not believe what he saw.

There were three armed warriors for each of his two hundred militias. He had been outnumbered and each of his soldiers was in shackles. Then General Besa realized that he had been hoodwinked.

"My wife's name is Chansa, and I have four children. Please tell them for me that I loved them," General Besa asked the person acting as Emperor Chiti III for a favor, and then he cut his own throat and slumped on the floor, dead.

General Chintu Chabala landed easily at Mungwi with his one hundred strong militias. When General Chabala entered the royal cottage, he found his wife and son chained to the poles.

The General was confused.

"*Dad*, please help me!" His son cried.

"Unchain me, Chintu, why did you do this to us?" His wife screamed.

Three hundred royal soldiers attacked the camp, shooting fiery arrows into the dry shrubs they had scattered all over the compound. The militias were ingulfed in flames and began to scamper in every direction for safety.

Many of them burned to death.

Those who survived were all arrested.

Stranded inside the royal cottage, General Chabala untied his wife and son and asked them to lift up their hands in surrender, and after kissing them goodbye, he pushed them outside of the royal cottage.

The ready warriors who were about to shoot stopped when their superior officer shouted, "Stop!"

Realizing that his wife and son were safe, General Chabala reached into his sheath for a blade, and he gave a deep slash to his trachea, and he laid dead in a pool of his own blood.

CHAPTER 8 | THE DEBACLE

When General Susula entered the royal palace at Ng'wena, there was nothing unassuming around. Everything went normally as always. Servants were tending to gardens, shepherds were taking care of animals, palace guards did not give General Susula a hard time entering the palace together with his fifty accompanying militias.

But one thing looked, and even sounded, off; things were too perfect for a normal day.

"Maybe it's because everyone is at *Ukusefya Pang'wena* annual ceremony," General Susula reassured himself.

In addition, Susula's spy at the palace remained quiet throughout the ordeal and he did not give the invading militias any warning.

The fifty strong army got stationed at every strategic corner of the palace according to the plan. Each of the fifty soldiers also carried a gun.

Exactly at each post one of the fifty militias stood, there were two or three royal warriors hiding.

So, as soon as each militia stood at their station according to the plan, someone cocked the gun, smiled, and ordered, "Bring your *ngwanis*," and all of them surrendered and were immediately shackled.

When General Susula entered the throne room, he was greeted by a full house, but not what anyone had expected. On the throne sat someone, tied to the throne legs, and facing away from the entrance of the room. There were people seated in the seats reserved for the *Kabilos* and *Chilolos*, tied and facing the wall.

General Susula ran towards the throne to see who was seated on the throne tied, and to his amazement, it was Rev. Baxter. And the entire committee from Mambweland was shackled to royal seats.

Strength left General Susula and like a boneless blob of flesh, he flopped to the ground. He was just about to point his own gun to this head and end it all when a sound rang from nowhere, "*Boom*!" and it knocked the gun off his hand. General Susula fell in one direction and his gun in the opposite direction.

"It's over, General," a familiar voice announced.

And when the downtrodden General turned and looked, it was none other than Colonel Yamfya.

"You, traitor!" General Susula shrieked.

"Save your breath, General," another familiar voice shouted from the doorway, leading a retinue that included the Regent Extraordinaire, the Queen Dowager, Susula's mother, the emperor, Nkole II, Chief Nsokolo II and a silhouette of the usual followers ranging from counsellors, officials, to courtiers.

What? How? I had them locked up, I mean General Kalyata and Nkole II. How did they escape? Traitors! They had insiders working with them…I should have known, General Susula struggled to reconcile his failed plan and the loose ends that had led to its failure as he mused.

***

Though failed, General Susula had marshaled the greatest collection of personnel so far in an attempt to overthrow the monarchy.

He had penetrated nearly every rank in the military using his former position as Deputy Supreme Commander and as prince.

He had a strong build-up of a militia strong enough to overrun any kingdom in the surrounding vicinity.

In addition to that, he had the support of one of the largest missionary organizations of the day, the White Fathers Mission of Central Africa (WFMCA). The CFMCA, through its headquarters in Mambweland, under the vicarship of Rev. Baxter, had supplied guns, logistical support, and personnel.

The plan's weak link was Chief Nsokolo II. He had feigned cooperation with the rebels and the WFMCA. He had participated in fanning the plan's flames and had offered his warriors to detain both

General Kalyata and Nkole II in his kingdom's dungeons. But unknown to the rebellion, he was acting on orders from the empire.

Few years prior, when the Regent Extraordinaire and Emperor Chiti III returned from the retreat at Kasama Lodge, they suspected that the traitor whom the disgraced priest, Father Ignatius, had alluded to was, in fact, General Susula, but they wanted to be sure.

So, they kidnapped General Susula's personal assistant, Colonel Kamfwa Yamgwa's family. They promised Colonel Yamfwa that his family would not only be released if he cooperated but that they would also give him lands and special privileges in the empire.

Colonel Yamfwa had revealed three facts that shook the monarchy to the core.

"Your Majesty…" Colonel Yamfwa had begun.

"We are listening."

"Please forgive me, what I am about to say is not good, not even for me uttering it before the sons of *Lesa*."

"What is it, Colonel, we know things that are hard to process. Come on, say it, we will not hold you accountable."

"First…" Colonel Yamfwa had looked timidly across the aisle where General Kalyata was seated drinking his mildly brewed *katata* in a copper goblet.

It was very clear to the royals and General Kalyata that what the Colonel wanted to say was very important. Therefore, they pepped him to say without fear or shame. They assured him that they were ready for anything.

"You can tell us anything, and we will not kill you as promised," Emperor Chiti III had reassured.

"Nkole II…"

"What about my son?" The Regent Extraordinaire had jumped in to interject.

"Let him say it, Father."

"Indeed, Your Majesty, give the Colonel a hedge," General Kalyata had chipped in.

Looking first at the Regent Extraordinaire and then at General Kalyata, Colonel Yamfwa ruptured, "Nkole II is not your biological son,

Your Majesty, but General Kalyata's."

The place where they were meeting went deathly silent.

No-one said a word.

No-one looked at another.

One could hear the movements of air in the room as heartbeats increased in their rhythms.

Then General Kalyata broke the silence, albeit only barely as he muttered lowly and mumbled drunkenly.

"This can't be, this can't be."

Regent Extraordinaire groaned.

"Ugh…what did you say? Can't even keep a secret?"

Emperor Chiti III sighed, and brawled with his own words, *"This is impossible."*

Colonel Yamfwa continued.

"Lady Kapambwe wanted her son to be prince, and that's the reason why she drugged and slept with you, Your Majesty, so that she could claim that you had impregnated her. She was already six weeks pregnant with General Kalyata's child at that time, but she didn't tell the General."

"General!" Emperor Chiti III

roared.

***

"Son, General Kalyata is not to blame here, your mother told me about the affair long time ago and I sanctioned it after the fact, but I am sure it has caught even the General by surprise regarding him being the father of Nkole II, isn't it so General?"

"Y...yes, Your Majesty."

"So, what do we do now, Father?"

"Nothing. I mean, nothing for now. We must hear what more the Colonel has to say, Son."

Chiti III remembered what his father had taught him about collecting as much intel as possible from enemies and friends alike.

He calmed himself.

The atmosphere had lightened up. Learning for the first time that the Regent Extraordinaire already knew about his affair with Lady Kapambwe but kept it to himself, unsettled General Kalyata, but got him thinking.

He just saved my life. All this time he

knew but said nothing. He was protecting, all along he was protecting me, and Lady Kapambwe, but why?

The Regent Extraordinaire turned towards General Kalyata and whispered in his ears, *Thank you, you had saved me from a gaping nightmare, don't dwell on it too much!*

"You said you had three things, what is the second?" Emperor Chiti III asked.

"Yes, Majesty," Colonel Yamfwa had responded, and continued.

"General Susula is planning to overthrow you, Your Majesty."

Then Colonel Yamfwa went on to explain in great detail how Susula had overheard the conversation between Lady Kapambwe and Nkole II. He further explained that Nkole II was as much a prisoner of Lady Kapambwe, "because when the prince became aware that you were not his father, he wanted to make everything official and concentrate on his boat-building profession. But Lady Kapambwe said that he was born to be king. She also blackmailed him that she would implicate his father, General Kalyata, in this…"

"In what?" General Kalyata asked, angrily.

"All I knew was that she was going to tell the emperor that it was *you* who hatched the idea of hiding Nkole II's true parentage."

"Blackmail, that sneaky *basilisk*, blackmailer!" Regent Extraordinaire screamed.

But not any one of them was ready for what was to come next. Both Regent Extraordinaire and Emperor Chiti III had been warned about it, but they had not expected that it would materialize to the level of direct confrontation.

"General Susula got guns and an army of fighters from Rev. Baxter and WFMCA, Sir!"

The last revelation hit the royal convocation very hard. The trio had decided to exercise utmost care and patience in order not only to quell the rebellion but to ensure that every culprit involved was brought to account.

"How do we suppress this, Father,

General Kalyata?" Emperor Chiti III asked.

"If I may speak, My Lords?" Colonel Yamfwa had requested.

"Go ahead," the emperor had granted.

"Chief Nsokolo…"

"What about him?" General Kalyata asked.

"He holds the key. General Susula and Rev. Baxter finally brought him to their sides after he had refused similar requests for a very long time. General Susula threatened to expose him to you and Rev. Baxter offered him guns and a promise to protect his realm."

"But for what reason, I mean, expose *him* for what?" Regent Extraordinaire had demanded to know.

"He broke the law, Sir. He's allowed slave trade in his kingdom and he's reestablished brothels. He's been violating other regulations you set up, for example, he's not provided the required quotas of military men to the imperial cache."

"*And it's General Susula who is responsible for the* Maluba Reforms *enforcement in the military*," General Kalyata remembered.

***

The convocation had resolved that it would first bring Chief Nsokolo to its side and ask him to play along with both General Susula and Rev. Baxter. He would appear to be cooperating while being the convocation's eyes.

General Kalyata was to also play along with General Susula's blackmail but not to disclose to Lady Kapambwe that the convocation was involved.

As General Susula's most trusted assistant, Colonel Yamfwa was tasked with the responsibility of recruiting soldiers who were loyal to the realm and to replace those who were anti-monarchy around General Susula.

He would be updating General Kalyata on every detail of the plan on a frequent basis. The convocation had also agreed to create a *double* for Emperor Chiti III and to only involve the Queen Dowager and the new Lady Chancellor Kasuba Kapasa after the scheme had picked up momentum.

CHAPTER 9 | TRIBUNAL

S cales for skin: It gathers, its skin protected by scales. There is tension in the air as it squeezes itself inside its scales, the Ground Pangolin, an animal, one of its kind in the world.

All animals in the world are covered by skin, not this one; it is the only animal covered by overlapping layers of scales.

It used to be young with youthful keratin. But now, it has grown, it has seen many bitter and better days. It has hardened scales, and it stretches itself hundreds of meters in spaces of between twelve and thirty-nine centimeters, respectively.

It will not go down easily, and its value is in its meat and scales – hard, medicinal, and tasty. It does not attack arbitrarily, but when it is attacked, it curls into a ball, with its tail scales protruding, pointed outside. It is ready to discharge its sharp-edged tails, hiss, and puff, and then, a shootout.

***

"All be seated, Reverend Morgan Helm Hubbard of the Christian Missionary Society (CMS) is presiding," Malaika Kopeka called the court to order.

Since the death of her mistress, Queen Matanda, in child labor, Malaika had given herself to the study of Christian thinking and philosophy and to learning the English language at the instruction of the previous emperor, His Majesty Chiti II, now the Regent Extraordinaire.

The new emperor, Chiti III, appointed Malaika as the palace clerk and registrar.

Rev. Baxter had demanded, "I will not accept the verdict of this court if I don't get a neutral adjudicator."

And the empire had decided to engage the CMS which, hitherto, had not established a mission station in Bembaland, to preside over the trial of the dissidents.

CMS had sent Rev. Hubbard.

"You're a missionary, Rev. Baxter, why did you feel it was your responsibility to overthrow a legitimate monarchy?" Hubbard asked.

"No comment."

"You supplied guns and a trained militia to the failed coup; do you admit or deny?"

"I will not comment."

"Was the British government involved in this?"

"No."

"Was the LMS involved in this?"

"No. I and my people are innocent. We welcomed General Susula in our midst just as we do anyone who wants to convert to the Christian faith."

"But testimonial evidence from the previous witnesses, especially the testimony of Colonel Yamfwa and Chief Nsokolo II clearly established that you were the mastermind?"

"That was a lie. We had provided guns for self defence, and not for their use in a mutiny."

"You provided over two hundred

guns all for self-defense, sir?"

"Yes."

"And just as conveniently those guns are found in the use to assassinate the emperor, was that just a coincidence?"

"I don't know, but what I know is that we did not insinuate or counsel dissidents."

"Do you have any last words?"

"Yes, I do. In time, not many years from now, you will all witness the landing of the eagles. Each shall land on the topmost crest and from there, dictate the Kingdom of our God and his Christ. At that time, the ignorant and brutal murders of this so-called empire will bow with their hands lifted up and willingly surrender to the army of redemption."

"What are you saying, Rev. Baxter? You mean England is planning to take possession of Africa?"

"That and more, Hon. Hubbard. I know that you, of the CMS are already facilitating that, how hypocritical of you!"

"Rev. Baxter, it's not me who is on

trial here, it is you who is alleged to have attempted to carry out a mutiny?"

"Ugh, you and I, Hon. Hubbard, are the same; we are here to civilize these pagans and to show them the way of salvation. Doing less than that is not worth a single float that made us triumph over the vicious storms and sea waves to reach here."

"Now you call them pagans, Rev. Baxter, and yet you gave them guns?"

"Well, they aren't Greeks, Romans, or Christians, so who are they?"

"They are humans, *humans*, Rev. Baxter!"

"Not to me, or at least, to *us*."

At that moment, there was noise inside the courtroom.

Everyone was fidgeting and whispering and saying something to one another.

The president of the meeting ordered everyone to be quiet, but no-one seemed to hear him.

Then his assistant, Malaika, raised her voice and ordered.

"The presiding judge says 'order'!"

Everyone heard her, and they,

indeed, stopped making noise.

The session resumed.

"Before the interruption, you said that *our* African counterparts are not humans, though I find that irrelevant to these proceedings here today, it interests me to think that you claim to be a pastor and yet you disregard a very simple proposition advanced through Genesis that God created all people in his image?"

"He created *humans* in his image, Mr. Hubbard, not these baboons."

"And by 'humans' you mean…"

"Whites, yes, Mr. Hubbard, Whites, and if you keep defending these, then you are not supporting the holy cause!"

Rev. Hubbard and Malaika looked at each other as if to agree that it was time for a verdict.

Immediately the president found Rev. Baxter and all his accomplices "guilty," there was a sustained applause which shot its spikes across the entire palace and outside where people were gathered waiting for the verdict.

And motioning to Emperor Chiti III, Rev. Hubbard, in a low, polite voice said, "Sentencing the guilty is your duty, Your Majesty."

Then he instructed Malaika to call the next matter.

"The next case is General Susula," Malaika announced.

The Queen Dowager, his own mother, was among those who testified against the disgraced rebel leader.

The trial did not last long before he was found guilty, together with those who plotted with him.

General Susula remained relatively composed and quiet for the most part of the trial, and even shed a tear when his mother testified that she warned him through a very well-known and familiar parable she had taught him since he was a child.

"I told him *'Don't not be sober,'* and he understood what I meant," she said.

But Susula had shown his anger when Yamfwa blabbed to the court against his former commander's indiscretions.

"Kamfwa. Traitor. Betrayer. You, *mulola kwakaba* (the one who pivots to where conditions become favorable). I will kill you. I will murder your entire clan!" General Susula avowed in a strong, angry voice.

"I have decided that Lady Kapambwe will be tried under the law of Chatindubwi, now Nkolemfumu, established by her own father, King Chimba, with King Nkole II presiding." Emperor Chiti III ordered.

There were some noises. Some shouted, "Try her by the superior law of Bembaland," but that was not sustained.

People were at least satisfied that the prime rebels – General Susula and Rev. Baxter – were found guilty.

Sentencing for the guilty would be announced the following week after the emperor had consulted the "elders, our customs and precedent."

The meeting was adjourned to the following day.

The crowd dispersed.

***

The meeting resumed.
Emperor Chiti III was presiding.

"I have consulted widely. Although Rev. Baxter is not native to these lands, he, nevertheless, became part of us by voluntarily accepting to work among our people. In that regard alone, it will not be wrong to sentence him by our customs and laws. But I went further than that and consulted on the law in *Ingalande* (England). There, too, they have laws, and if a person rebels against the monarchy or the state, he is punished by death. Rev. Baxter will be paraded together with his guilty accomplices at Mbala Grove and shot until pronounced dead. Their bodies shall be buried at sea as is the practice of those who travel."

The crowd shouted, "Wisdom. Wisdom!"

The next to be sentenced were General Susula and his fellow rebels. Malaika motioned to the crowd to keep quiet. She called on the Queen Dowager to announce the emperor's sentence.

"General Susula is my own flesh and blood. He is the Regent Extraordinaire's own son, and brother to our emperor. But he plotted to kill the emperor and to exile both his father and me. Emperor Chiti III orders that former general, Susula Mulenga Chiti, be executed by shooting seven arrows into his heart until he is pronounced dead. The sentence will be carried out in Mambweland at the auspices of Chief Nsokolo II. He should be buried in a common grave, and not at Milemba."

As he heard his mother's announcement, Susula shed thick tears.

His mother cried, too.

Then Susula shouted, "What did you expect me to do? You love a child who was not your own blood better than me. You worship that stupid blind of a father who is full of mistrust for the *foreigners*. I asked you to make me emperor, your own son, and you refused."

As for the fifty and the warriors who flopped at Kalungu River and Mungwi, together totaling two hundred and sixteen, they were to be shot dead and buried in a mass grave in an unspecified location.

***

Things had returned to normal in Bembaland and at the palace. Emperor Chiti III was again seated on his throne adjudicating regular affairs and receiving reports.

"Next, what is your report?"

"I am from Nkolemfumu. Lady Kapambwe was sentenced to death and was provided with poison in drink. She is deceased."

"Next, what is your report?"

"I am from Mambweland. General Susula escaped. He was rescued by Christian fighters."

"Wha…what?"

***

What followed was a frenzy, a zipped collaboration of many words into silence.

The emperor's crown almost fell to the ground.

Courtiers and officials stood still like monuments.

Business ended abruptly.

It was as if the sun had risen from the west and set through the east.

"What did you say? I mean, I heard you."

Emperor Chiti III was visibly perturbed.

Both the Regent Extraordinaire and the Queen Dowager had retired at Mpulamasanga Lodge. And the royal vacation lodge was right in Mambweland.

And the emperor remembered.

"Father. Mother! *Kapaso*, call General Kalyata, immediately!"

CHAPTER 10 | THE FUGITIVE

Way of a river horse. Call it a hippo, it moves close to the podium in order to hear as the last of the reformers laid in state. It is huge, with fearsome tusks which it flaunts remarkably as it looks for space with a clear view.

It is in a hurry, squeezing aggressively to tangle with two dead crocodiles now paraded in cowhides. With its bulky body on stumpy legs, it prides itself on its strength contained in its gigantic head to bully its way to the top.

Today, it will thrust its short tail, and four toes on each of its feet in the direction of Milemba to showcase its hide, meat, and ivory tusks.

It will shelter the late royals from purgatory by fortifying its dense body underneath the water, leaving its ears, eyes, and nostrils, located high on the head, to keep a good view of dangers and to survive the perilous conditions that challenge its nature, territory, and future.

Adaptation, steadiness, tool orientation and ability to live in water and on land, make this water horse one of the most daring water-land animals in the world.

***

General Mporokoso must assess the viability of climbing the mountain in order to hunt the fugitive general who was now being aided by Christian militias equipped with guns.

The only advantage General Mporokoso had was that he outnumbered the dissident forces by three to one.

"General, we lost the pontoon bridge at Bolabola. And all our seventy warriors are dead." The first report stated.

"General, Commander Mutanshi has been defeated, sir. And all of his seventy-eight warriors cannot be accounted for." The second report stated.

"General, we …"

"Stop right there, I don't have any more strength to stomach another loss," General Mporokoso disrupted the third reporter.

"But sir…"

"But what, lieutenant, I…I am tired of these…"

"I have good news, sir," the third reporter pushed his way and prevented the general from completing his sentence.

"Hmm…hmm, say it?"

"Our vanguard led by Commander Mboloma has spotted the dissident Susula at Ibenga Mission. They say that he is armed and dangerous and he is surrounded by about three hundred Christian soldiers."

"That is both bad and good news. *Colonel Pinto*, send a homing pigeon with a message to General Kalyata that I need reinforcement. If I don't hear from him within an hour, I will go and kill him myself."

"Sure, sir."

***

It was more than one hour, and no response had come from the God of War. It so happened that Susula had a spy inside General Mporokoso's regiment, and the bird had been shot dead, so it never delivered the missive to General Kalyata.

It was now going to be two hours.

"*Colonel Pinto*, how long can it take to send a calvary warrior to General Kalyata's bunker at Chief Nsokolo's palace?"

"At least three and a half, General."

"Forget it. Bring my uniform and my *mfuti* and my horse. Have the following accompany me: General Chileshe Fyebo, Commander Mukuka Nkula, Officer Cadet Chembo, Lieutenant Sampa, Lieutenant Mushitu, and yourself. Come on, let us go!"

With the exception of Lieutenant Mushitu, everyone mentioned was ready waiting for General Mporokoso.

"Is everyone here, Colonel Pinto?" General Mporokoso asked.

"Yes, sir, except for Lieutenant

Mushitu."

"That is not everyone, Colonel, Mushitu is not here, get him quickly."

"Yes, sir."

Colonel Pinto went first to Lieutenant Mushitu's hut, but the lieutenant was not there. He ran to check at the cafeteria, and the lieutenant was not there, either.

Just when he was about to give up, on his way to reporting to General Mporokoso, Lieutenant Mushitu emerged from the bushes.

"God…oh, I was answering the call of nature," Lieutenant Mushitu explained himself.

"Pull yourself together quickly, we are going," ordered Colonel Pinto.

"But where to, Colonel?"

"To kill that lunatic of a prince."

General Mporokoso rode on his horse alone. The rest bumped themselves inside a carriage. There was no particular paved route to Ibenga Mission.

They rode through hills and valleys and impassable jungles.

But they were determined to

conquer the rough terrain and reach the destination before the dissidents had a chance to flee.

Suddenly, a small piece of papyrus escaped Lieutenant Mushitu's hand due to the bumpy path and it fell right in front of Colonel Pinto's right leg. Not paying attention to its content, Colonel Pinto handed it over to Lieutenant Mushitu. No-one would have cared except for the manner in which Mushitu behaved when he got it back.

No-one said a word.

Halfway through the journey to Ibenga Mission, General Mporokoso stopped the carriage for a strategy session.

As they deliberated, Lieutenant Mushitu sneaked out and was unaccounted for.

Colonel Pinto, whose role was communication and running General Mporokoso's small errands, trailed Mushitu to a nearby bushel where Mushitu was trying to send a homing message to Susula.

"I had suspected you, but I didn't expect you to be a mole," Pinto said when he caught Mushitu in the act.

Mushitu attacked Pinto and a fight ensued. In the subsequent scuffle, Mushitu accidentally pulled a trigger, and *Kaboom*! Pinto went silent.

Everyone at the strategy table heard the gun shot.

"What was that? *Chembo*, go and check. Be careful," General Mporokoso commanded.

After a few minutes, Chembo returned, carrying an almost lifeless body of Pinto on his shoulders.

Commander Nkula, who was trained in military medics found a faint pulse on Pinto.

"He's still alive. Who did this to you?" Commander Nkula tried to inquire.

"M-u-s-h i-s…a m-o…"

But before Pinto could not complete his sentence, he succumbed to death due to the bullet lodged in his chest.

"He's dead…" Nkula began, "I think he was trying to say that Mushitu was a mole."

"General Fyebo, you specialize in investigations?"

"Yes, General Mporokoso."

"Go back to the crime scene. Find me something, anything that can provide a clue to what happened there?"

"Yes, sir."

***

It didn't take more than ten minutes, General Chileshe Fyebo was back.

He had a piece of papyrus in his hand.

"Sir, you were right. Mushitu was a mole. He was trying to warn Susula of our coming. What shall we do now?"

"We go, now, before he reaches there. He will be on foot."

The group galloped as fast as they could.

Just before sunset they arrived at Ibenga Mission in Mambweland.

Disguised as Christian militias, General Mporokoso's men infiltrated the mission security details.

Sir, we have a problem, Nkula whispered in General Mporokoso's left ear.

"What is it, Commander?"

"It seems they have *them*, General."

"Who is them?"

"The former emperor and the queen. They are held captive in the room next to where Susula is meeting the Christian generals."

"Not again," General Mporokoso was disappointed.

"What options do we have, General? Should we wait until they go to bed?"

"We can't, by then Mushitu might have arrived, and he will alert them. *Change of mission.* We must rescue the royals first, and hopefully by then General Kalyata would have arrived. Did Chembo send the missive?"

"Yes, sir."

***

What followed was a daring mission.

Pretending to be a servant and delivering food and drink to the captives, Cadet Officer Chembo entered the captives' room.

As he offered the former emperor food, he softly whispered, *I bring you greetings from General Mporokoso, Your Majesty.*

The former emperor in turn whispered to his wife, *We've got good company, my love.*

***

The mission initially went smoothly.

The two royals were dressed in Christian gowns and sneaked through the back door.

They were just about to whisker them away in a ready chariot when Mushitu arrived, panting heavily from running nonstop.

"General, General, *they* are here, somewhere…" and Mushitu fainted.

"Protect General Susula," a voice announced and put the soldiers on security alert.

A military guard came running and sweating, "General, they are gone, the royal captives are gone!"

Mporokoso's men exchanged fire with the Christian soldiers.

General Mporokoso continued running to safety taking the royals with him as Lieutenant Sampa covered them by shooting back at the Christian soldiers chasing them.

As General Mporokoso put the former queen inside the carriage, he just heard a prodding sound, "Ouch! That really hurts."

General Mporokoso then realized that the sound was coming from the former emperor who was just a breath away from him.

"Just hold on, Majesty, we will be out of harm's way very soon."

And before he could blink General Mporokoso heard a howl of pain and anguish coming from Lieutenant Sampa who was covering him.

Then it was quiet.

"Oh, no!" General Mporokoso wailed.

He knew that something awful had happened to his comrade, but he had to rescue the royals from danger first.

After ascertaining that they were safely away from danger, the general ordered the chariot to stop.

"You are hurt, Your Majesty. You have been shot in your back with a poisoned arrow, Sir."

"How long before the poison filters?" Regent Extraordinaire asked.

"Do not worry, Sir. Commander Nkula will perform first aid, and this will revive you until we reach Chief Nsokolo's village."

CHAPTER 11 | END OF AN ERA

After leaving the royals with a traditional herbalist named Kafwanka at headman Kantumoya's village in Mambweland who extracted the poison from the Regent Extraordinaire, General Mporokoso decided to leave the rest of the crew there to guard the royals.

He only took Officer Cadet Chembo with him.

"*General Mporokoso*, the empire will not forget your sacrifice," Queen Dowager reassured.

"I…I am only doing my job, Ma'am."

"A…and…you don't need to return to Ibenga, General. Susula must have escaped by now."

"General Kalyata taught me not to leave a colleague on the battlefield. If not to catch Susula, I must bring the body of Lieutenant Sampa back to Ng'wena, Majesty, Sir."

***

On the way back to Ibenga Mission, General Mporokoso and Officer Cadet Chembo met a cheerful convoy of a detachment under General Chansa returning with the body of General Susula.

Just after the rescue of the royals, General Chansa's detachment with the help of an Arab contingent acting on General Kalyata's orders, had pursued the Christian soldiers who were fleeing with General Susula.

An unidentified Arab soldier had shot General Susula in the head and he died instantly.

When they had realized that General Susula was dead, the Christian soldiers had abandoned the mission and scampered in different directions for cover.

Many of them were also arrested and were being transported to Ng'wena in the caravan.

"As our troops mopped up the last pockets of resistance, we stumbled upon the body of Lieutenant Sampa and we have him with us here, General," General Chansa reported.

"Thank you, General Chansa. Now I need to go and fetch the body of Colonel Pinto which we left hidden under a cliff."

"Rest, General Mporokoso. You're a hero, sir. I heard what you did for the royals. You're the star of the operation. I will have my troops go and fetch Colonel Pinto."

"I am *not* a hero, sir. I was only doing my duty. But I appreciate the offer of retrieving the colonel's body. Thank you!"

CHAPTER 12 | ALLIANCES

Emperor Chiti III presided over the death of his father and adopted mother. He had allowed their corpses to lie in state for seven days at Ng'wena. Thousands of people paid tribute and on the last day before burial at Milemba. Seer Kakunga invited Shimwalule, Changala Kabotwe II, to introduce the emperor.

"As my last duty, I now invite His Lordship Kabotwe II to perfect the rite."

Kabotwe II, a lanky, dark figure with a shanty command of respect, stood up, nodded his gratitude to the seer and took a bamboo podium erected for that purpose.

"Thank you, Hon. Kakunga. It is my rare honor and pleasure to ask His Majesty, King of kings and protector of the forest. Your Majesty your people await."

Emperor Chiti III stood up and

walked past the two cowhides in which the lifeless bodies of his father and mother were wrapped.

He had been told of the triumph of the joint forces of the Arab-assisted reinforcement of General Chansa's company and of the Mporokoso-led daring mission that rescued his father and mother.

Shortly before his father passed, he, together with Lady Kasuba, the Chancellor, had arrived at herbalist Kafwanka's infirmary at headman Kantumoya's village.

His father's health had deteriorated because of the type of poison used which Kafwanka said was "not common. It seems to have originated from the land of the *foreigners*. We don't have this snake venom here."

Despite every effort made, the situation could not be salvaged.

When he saw his son, Regent Extraordinaire held him in his hands and said, "Son, my time is here. Take good care of your mother and the empire. Everything you need to succeed I have taught you. Remember, be a…"

"…a successful emperor rather than a wise one only," Emperor Chiti III had completed his father's sentence.

The emperor had then placed a finger before his father's pursed lips to hush him, saying, "Don't talk, preserve your energy, Father. I have sent for the royal physician, and he will be here soon."

Then it was quiet.

Very quiet.

The Queen Dowager was in another room preparing a bow of hot soup for her ailing husband when she heard the emperor whispering into Lady Kasuba's ears, "Don't let her know for now. It will not be easy to receive double bad news, the death of her husband and that of her son."

At that point, the Queen Dowager knew that her husband and son were no more.

She reached into her purse for a tiny bottle of a reddish-blue liquid, sneaked in when no-one was paying attention and hugged the lifeless body of her husband, and then she went to sleep.

When the emperor found both his

parents clasped together, he remarked, "*They* stayed together in death, just as they did in life!"

***

At their funeral, he walked to the podium with the memory of how they passed away fresh in his mind. He took the elevated stage and began to speak:

> The deaths of my father and of the Queen Dowager put an end to an era. An era that began with intense reforms pioneered by the then Lady Maluba, now lying here in state.
>
> This I promise that under my continued reign, I shall not shudder away from one of their reforms and I will carry them out to their completion.
>
> And today, before we give them their final rest, I make four more additional reforms based on the wisdom I received from my father while he was the Regent Extraordinaire.
>
> The first additional reform is that only members of the Bemba Royal Clan, the *Miti* (Tree) Clan, can contest for emperor position, which from hence shall be termed the

120

"Chitimukuluship."

This is to ensure that there is only a limited number of people who could vie for succession. This will also lessen succession disputes after the death of a Chitimukulu, beginning with my death.

Second, and with immediate effect, I am appointing the following members of the Miti Clan to chiefly positions, and these shall constitute my inner Cabinet and confirmed contenders for the Chitimukuluship when the reigning Chitimukulu dies without a successor: Chiefs Nkula, Mwamba, Nkole, Makasa, Chikwanda, and Mporokoso.

Third, I am abolishing the role of the *Chilolo* in debating succession and the strangling of the ailing emperor. Tradition has been that a *Chilolo* finds an opportune moment to strangle the Chitimukulu so that he dies without pain. Such a practice is now proscribed. Like my father, a Chitimukulu shall be allowed to die when their natural time is up.

Fourth, from now onwards, only the Chitimukulu shall preside over religious and ritual matters. With immediate effect, the Office of the Spiritual Advisor will no longer be in existence.

Last, and with great honor and deference, I have asked General Kalyata, the God of War, to step down as Supreme Commander of the warriors of Bembaland. In his place, I am appointing Chief Mporokoso, who from whence shall assume the title Commander General Mporokoso.

The Honorable Sebela, now old and frail, writing for the historical royal records said, "Indeed, it was the end of an era. The end has started, but the beginning is yet to end."

***

The government of Chiti III began with the strengthening of existing alliances and the creation of new ones. Lady Kasuba, the emperor's aunt, and Chancellor of the empire stood up and made the announcement.

"All gathered except the emperor, stand *mukwai* (please). Enters Chief Matanda II, paramount chief of the Aushi people to offer his greetings and pay tribute to Emperor Chiti, the third."

"Greetings, Your Majesty, from the

traditional house from Chembe, Milengi, Samfya to Mansa. I bring you greetings from the land of *ubwaushi* (groundnuts), and in these delicately weaved baskets are the surpluses gathered from the just ended annual, magnificent *Chabuka Ceremony* – find beans, groundnuts and cassava to flavor and enrich the empire. Your Partner."

Emperor Chiti III stood up and nodded, and again sat down.

The Lady Chancellor stood up and made the second announcement.

"All gathered except the emperor, stand *mukwai*. Enters Chief Kopa III, paramount chief of the Bisa people to offer his greetings and pay tribute to Emperor Chiti, the third."

"Greetings, Your Majesty, from the traditional house of Umupika (Mpika) all the way to Icinsali (Chinsali). I bring you greetings from the lands where we celebrate the famous and invigorating *Chinamanongo Ceremony* – please find our skillfully hunted and preserved game meat. Your Partner."

Emperor Chiti III stood up and nodded, and again sat down.

The Lady Chancellor stood up and made the third announcement.

"All gathered except the emperor, stand *mukwai*. Enters Chief Mushota III, paramount chief of the Chishinga people to offer his greetings and pay tribute to Emperor Chiti, the third."

"Greetings, Your Majesty, from the traditional house at Kawambwa. I bring you greetings from the lands where we celebrate the fishful and deliciously *Chishinga Malaila Ceremony* – please find our famed and palatably salted fishes prepared just for this occasion. Your Partner."

The Lady Chancellor stood up and made the fourth announcement.

"All gathered except the emperor, stand *mukwai*. Enters Deputy Chief Chembo, acting as proxy for his mother, Her Highness, Chieftainess Chembo Kasako Chimbala from the lake area called *Kashiba Kabena Mofya* (a well where the Mofya Clan dwells), to offer greetings and pay tribute to Emperor Chiti, the third."

"Your Majesty, from the traditional house of the Mofya Clan. I bring you greetings from my mother, now too old to travel and barely blind, from the lands where we celebrate the legendary *Chabalankata Traditional Ceremony* – please accept our copper and ivory. Mother confirms this partnership and confers longevity to Your Majesty."

As Lady Chancellor was about to invite Chief Mambwe of the Cunda (Kunda) people, an emissary came forward, crawling on his knees and incessantly bowing before the emperor, and he whispered into the Chancellor's ears.

"Our kraal has just been attacked by the Nguni troopers. Senior Headman Mambwe has been abducted and his people are asking for your help."

The Lady Chancellor beckoned to Kabwe to approach and Kabwe was given the message she had received from Senior Headman Mambwe.

The emperor gestured to the Chancellor to suspend the announcements for a while. The emperor then called Commander General Mporokoso and delegated to him to immediately send a company and save one of his vassal enclaves from the Nguni raiders.

"Yes, Majesty, straightaway, your wish is my command."

The General delegated the company stationed at Safwa Rapids with clear instructions: "To save the headman and his kraal, destroy the bandits and return with victorious news for His Majesty."

"Yes, Commander General."

With that having been taken care of, Lady Chancellor, with the permission of the emperor, returned to her list and continued where she had ended.

The fifth on the list were four Ng'umbo chiefs who were Senior Chief Mwewa, Chief Chitembo, Chief Mulongwe and Chief Mwansakombe. They offered their greetings and paid tribute with four boats and seventy-nine reed-weaved fishing baskets.

Simultaneously as the Chancellor was calling upon the combined dancing troupe made up of the Swaka, Tabwa and Unga with their Bemba counterparts to dance to *Imbeni* drumbeat, a messenger came with a private message for Chief Makasa.

Chief Makasa Chisenga excused himself and stepped outside to listen to the messenger.

"Your Highness, I bring you good news from Stevenson Road Parish in eastern Mambweland."

"And which is?" Chief Makasa inquired.

"Bishop Dupont would like to meet you at your earliest opportune, sir."

"Sure, tell the newly arrived bishop to wait for me at our usual spot."

The messenger left.

Chief Makasa prepared to return to the Assembly to rejoin the royals in the celebrations and speeches.

As he walked towards the chamber which housed the Assembly, Chief Makasa was in high spirits.

Yes, I finally will get to drown this boy in his own soil. If everything goes well, with the help of the Christian, I will be the soul emperor of Ulubemba. *My philosophy is tolerance. My style is gain without sweat.*

Chief Makasa was welcomed back inside just when the courtier-servants were passing around goblets of mildly brewed *kachasu* (local whiskey).

Chief Mwamba who was seated next to Chief Kapasa noticed that his neighbor was all smiles, and Mwamba pricked a rhetorical question.

"It's rule and drink, Brother?"

Without even gazing at his friend, Chief Makasa responded with a nod and a proverb, "Yes, Brother. *Ubucenjeshi bumo, pamo no kupusa* (once beaten, twice shy)!"

Chief Mwamba interpreted this to mean that it was an advantage to be both on the Chief's Council and to drink beer.

Then Chief Mwamba responded with his own proverb, *Kolwe angala pa musambo anasha* (literally, "A monkey plays safely on a familiar tree branch," which could mean that, "When you're in good terms one with another, you can play it safe.")

CHAPTER 13 | CIRCLE AT NKULA

Ndalasha Totilo was a forty-year-old bachelor who had been known to all the villagers at Chief Nkula's village. He had served in the reserve military command near Safwa Rapids since he was eighteen years old.

He was honorably discharged from the warrior guards.

Two years after his discharge, there was a spurt of attempted and sexual assaults on young girls aged between sixteen and seventeen in Nkula's village.

Girls who survived the assault described him as an imposing figure of about six feet tall with a bald head and wearing a burgundy jumper over khaki trousers. The matter was brought to village headman, Mukule, who instituted an investigation. The investigation led directly to Ndalasha Totilo. Ndalasha was referred to the chief's court for prosecution.

***

"We have gathered adequate evidence linking Ndalasha Totilo to a number of assaults sexual in nature around the Nkula's village. We have lined up four young girls, one was assaulted and three of them barely escaped," Headman Mukule presented his opening arguments before Chief Nkula.

"What do you say to these allegations, Ndalasha Totilo?" Chief Nkula asked.

"I am innocent. I can't remember committing such crimes. I did it, hmm, wait, I only did it in my sleep," Ndalasha gave a rambling statement.

Chief Nkula turned towards Headman Mukule and whispered in his ears.

"Is the accused of a sound mind?"

"Yes, Your Highness. He was honorably discharged from the warrior…."

Chief Nkula injected.

"You mean, he is a warrior?"

"He was. He's no longer one."

"Even so, Your Worship. Under the *Maluba Reforms* such matters lie to the Royal Court. It's beyond my jurisdiction."

The *Totilo case* was referred to the Royal Court.

***

And standing before Emperor Chiti III, Ndalasha Totilo was assigned a royal counselor, Mukwai Kabaso, to defend him. Mukwai stood and began advocacy in defence of Ndalasha Totilo.

"Your Majesty…"

The emperor stood up. Everyone stood. Then the emperor asked for his special banjo to be brought so that he could play it.

And they did.

"Mukwai?"

"I am here, Your Majesty!"

"Arrange a circle. Take Ndalasha back to Headman Mukule's kraal. Let them seek the solution from our customs."

"Yes, Your Majesty."

No-one dared to question the emperor's order. However, those present admired the judicious observation and discernment of the emperor.

"He gazed at Ndalasha for a little while and then he seemed disinterested," one elderly man commented.

"I think the emperor is a merciful and wise ruler," another man said.

"But these allegations are serious, can our customary system fix such behavior," a thirty-two-year-old palace cleaner who overheard the emperor's order whispered to himself.

***

"Mofya Musonda, you go first," Headman Mukule ordered.

There were about sixteen people sitting around a circle. Their ages ranged from sixteen years old to over-seventy years old. They had been chosen for their wisdom and positive community contributions. Ndalasha Totilo was siting alone in the middle of the circle. Mofya stood up and spoke.

"Ndalasha, you may not have remembered me. But I was barely nine years old, and I struggled to carry the bundle of firewood my mother had assigned to me. You showed up from nowhere and caried it for me to my house."

There was a small pause. Then Headman Mukule invited Musole Mbushi to speak.

"Ndalasha, to me you're a hero. When we faced a stalemate from the Nguni attackers at Samfya, you picked me up because I couldn't run; I was glazed by a spear and, thus, *this* limp.

You climbed the hill with me on your back till you reached a safe zone and handed me over to the command physician. Thank you!"

Ndalasha Totilo coiled himself in the middle of the circle as if he was attempting to bury himself in the ground. Headman Mukule shouted.

"Ndalasha! Pay attention!"

Then a sweet female voice interrupted. It was Ndalasha's mother, Sefelina. She was not part of the Circle, but she had been lurking in the concourses.

"May I…Your Worship, may I say something?"

Sefelina did not wait for Headman Mukule to respond, and she spoke.

"My son is a good person. He had served our empire honorably. And he had been a good, obedient son since his childhood, but…"

"But what, say it," Headman Mukule prompted.

"But since he returned from the camp, he's been behaving strangely, almost weird, at times…"

"Hmm, continue," Headman Mukule prompted further.

"He talks to himself, Your Worship."

"You mean in his sleep, that's normal."

"No, Your Worship. He talks to himself while wide awake."

"How so?"

"Sometimes, he shrieks as if he wants the ground to swallow him. I have even heard him shout, 'Save me, don't cut my leg.'"

There was a long pause.

A young woman of about thirty years old who was slated to go third stood up and gestured to Headman Mukule to allow her to speak. The headman simply nodded with his head.

"My name is Mungole Pembe. Ndalasha, as far as I am concerned, has never had a girlfriend. I am, probably, the closest he has ever had to a girlfriend. During the time I knew him, he always treated me kindly and with respect. Although I loved him and wanted him to be my boyfriend, he was always shy and did not acknowledge my love. My family gave me away to another man as a wife. My husband died in battle. I hear that it was Ndalasha who brought his body home for burial."

There was total silence.

Ndalasha began to cry.

"I never meant to harm any of the girls. Please help me. *It* wants to destroy me. *It* is a monster…"

Headman Mukule spoke next.

"Sefelina, what is *it*?"

"That was what I was trying to say. He calls it a monster and when it comes upon him, he gets extremely fearful. Your Worship, my son is innocent; he needs help."

There was an instant agreement among the members of the Circle, as they called the interactive court system.

Those who were scheduled to speak next agreed to forfeit their comments; they all answered, "Yes," to a general question posed by the headman: "Does everyone agree that Ndalasha is a good person?"

They further agreed that Ndalasha Totilo was suffering from some form of a post trauma stress disorder. They recommended that he should see a healer to cure his mind and soul.

"I will stay with him until the healer pronounces him healed," Mungole Pembe offered.

"I will bring him food everyday," Mulungu Bowa, an elderly widow, promised.

"I will take care of his farm, so he doesn't starve," a man shouted from the Circle.

Both the members of the Circle and the audience came and surrounded Ndalasha Totilo hugging him and heaping continuous praise for the things that he had said and done.

Then Mbereshi came forward.

She beckoned to everybody to leave Ndalasha alone for a little while. Everyone understood and gave her space. She lovingly hugged Ndalasha, pouring tears of benevolence on his neck.

"I know now that you didn't mean it; you're a good man," she poured out her heart to him.

"I am so sorry, *Sister.*"

"No need to, I know now. You didn't mean to rape me. It was the monster inside troubling you. Now, you will be fine, you will be healed."

"No, Sister. That's not a good excuse for my behavior…"

Mbereshi put her finger on Ndalasha's mouth.

"Shh! Keep your voice down! Just promise me."

Then Mbereshi took the palm of Ndalasha's right hand, deliberately directing it towards her protruding belly and pouring out tears of joy, and then she let it off.

"Do you promise me that you will help me raise your child; I am pregnant!"

Ndalasha could not contain his joy.

"I…I will, oh, *Sister*!"

The people heard the conversation.

The crowd, organically, morphed into a jamboree of cerebrations.

People brought food, alcohol, and drums.

They beat the drums and danced all night.

And when he was tired and retiring to bed, Headman Mukule sighed deeply.

"Our emperor is such a man of grand wisdom; he's turned a bitter herb into a sweet remedy!"

CHAPTER 14 | NGUNI MASSACRE

"Dad, those women are bleeding and they are in pain, their extremities are swelling around the gardens. At least send out some medicine men to attend to them."

There was tension – great tension.

"Wena weNdlovu, my son, I, Headman Mpisane, of the Gumbi Clan, follow in the footsteps of my great ancestors, from maXhosa, to Mandebele, and to maZulu. *Raid* and *brutality* are in our blood."

"Yes, Dad, but you could have just taken their headman, their food and implements, why did you also take their women and children?"

"Oh, my ordained successor, my naïve child. *Bembas are thieves*. They had nothing when they came to these lands. All they have now, they raided from us and other tribes. What has been our custom is to take away everything they store from us, with interest."

"Dad, are their women and children part of the interest?"

"Yes, Son. The Nc'wala Ceremony is around the corner. Headquarters at Mutenguleni is getting ready to glorify the King of kings, His Highness, King Mpezeni. I want to secure my position as head of the headmen through a generous offering."

"My, my, my, you're a strategist, Dad. What is more important than offering another headman?"

"You got it, Son. One headman for another, except with additional fringe benefits…"

"Of their women, children and animals!"

Just when the father and his son were discussing the spoils, the headman's chief informant arrived with disturbing news.

"Your Worship. May I enter?"

"Yes, Jere Nxumalo. What is it that brings you here, sweating?"

"There is a problem, sir."

"Say it, Dad is listening," Wena intruded.

"Safwa Rapids is coming, Your Worship."

"Wha…what? That is Chiti's regiment?"

"Yes, sir. But we didn't know that Senior Headman Mambwe had pledged fealty to the emperor."

"If he owes fealty to the emperor, we are in trouble. King Mpezeni has warned not to provoke the Bemba Empire until we are ready. This means that I am on my own."

There was another knock on the door. But even before they answered, a human head was thrown inside the tent, blooded and fresh.

"What…what is this…oh, my god, it's Mazyopa. Mazyopa, my daughter. Who did this to you? And you, Mpyuisani, my wife's…"

With a big, intimidating voice and a long-barbed spear in his left hand, a Bemba warrior forced his way into the tent and interrupted the dirge of the grieving headman.

"I did. I am *General Mponde*. Mponde Kapaya. We've taken our revenge."

"B-but, sir, I didn't know that…"

"…it's too late. You either kill yourself with this spear or I will feed your live body to hungry wolves."

"No, sir. I will return Headman Mambwe and give the emperor six hundred goats, one hundred cattle and fifty slaves. Please, sir. Spare our lives."

"Too late. Headman Mambwe has already been rescued; he's on his way home as I speak. As for your other offers, my soldiers have already barricaded your pavilion and uprooted everything. I know this is your son. He will die before you."

General Mponde did not mince words. As he was making declarations, his warriors were already apprehending Wena weNdlovu.

And in a blink of an eye, Wena's head was chopped off.

"Oh, my Wena weNdlovu. My Mazyopa. These brutes, you…"

And before Headman Mpisane could complete blurting out epithets, his head met the thin, sharp edge of General Mponde's sword.

There was no sound.

Only three human heads separated from their bodies.

"Our job here is done. *Corporal Malenga*?"

"Yes, sir!"

"Wrap these heads in honey and take them to Lord General Commander."

"Yes, sir."

Corporal Malenga rushed to his carriage, hastening to report to General Mporokoso. The note that accompanied an ersatz casket read, in part: *"As ordered by His Majesty, the job is done. The raider is gone, and so does his entire family and tribe. There are no further threats on the southern borders…"*

***

"They are dead, Ma'am, dead, brutally murdered by those *thieves* of Bembas."

The heavily wounded Nkosana returned from the scene of the carnage where she only survived by feigning death.

"Hold on in there, Nkosana. You must live. You're the only one I have now. I will treat you. You will be fine."

The wife of the dead Headman Mpisane, Tendai, fumed with fury as she attempted to calm Nkosana down, her last surviving servant.

Tendai, nicknamed, "The Morning Staress," was an epitome of beauty, perfection, and grace. She walked with the strut of a peacock in its prime, carrying a pawpaw-shaped bottom unto her two tiny feet, barely hanging onto a thinned waistline.

Her avocado-shaped full mooned face laid gracefully on an elongated neckline, adorned by some infectious eyelids standing straight as if on alert to the hazel-colored eye framework she termed, "My Hollows."

She was lovely to behold, impossible to ignore, and delicate to handle.

She had been betrothed to the now dead headman at the tender age of nine, got married to him at fourteen, and by the time she was sixteen years old, she had given birth to his two now-beheaded children, Wena weNdlovu and Mazyopa.

At twenty-four years of age, she had now lost the two tender loves of her life, Wena was barely nine years old and Mazyopa would have been eight in two days' time if she had not been brutally killed.

As of that terrible day, however, Tendai looked dejected, deflected, and tatty.

Her servant, Nkosana, was badly injured as she tried to escape the brutality of the Bemba warriors. Her entrails were barely holding outside her belly and her back had an x-ed cut driving deeply across it by a poisoned spear.

She was dying.

She died right in Tendai's hands.

"Revenge," she cried, *"I will revenge you, my Mpisane. My son, Wena. My daughter, Mazyopa!"*

Tendai remembered how the day began just like any other. She had woken up early, braving through the heavy dew with Mpyuisani, her servant, accompanied by two brave Nguni warrior guards.

It was turning out to be a bright, sunny day.

144

Trees looked happy, and the leaves danced uncontrollably to the tune of a fine westerly warm wind.

They had reached the cassava gardens which they had seized from the previous occupants of the area, the Ng'umbo people, whom they had driven far north.

Then by the early evening, just before sunset, a bloody, wounded warrior had come, warning her that, "The village has been raided, Headman Mambwe rescued, and the *monsters* are now headed towards your kraal."

Before she could process that news, another emissary had arrived, "Ma'am, they are all dead, I don't know about your family…"

Tendai had fainted at that moment.

Mpyuisani helped to recuperate her.

She had wanted to go back to the village to check on her family by herself. The two guards prevented her. Mpyuisani offered, instead, to go for her.

Mpyuisani never made it back.

She was beheaded together with Headman Mpisane, Wena, and Mazyopa.

Nkosana was preparing the evening meal when she was hacked down with a poisoned spear. The Bemba warrior thought that she

145

had died. But she barely survived and crawled her way to inform the mistress.

I must reach her. I must inform her, Nkosana had thought, while barely hanging on to her life.

Then left hopelessly alone, without food, water, or shelter, only with one of the surviving guards, Mwisange, Tendai headed towards the inferno – to Ng'wena itself. At nineteen years of age, Mwisange was already a rising star in the Nguni nation, destined to join King Mpezeni's elite guard because of his superior martial arts and people skills.

"Let's go, Mwisange."

And then she whispered to herself, "*I must avenge them. Heir for heir, blood for blood!*"

CHAPTER 15 | CATALYST

C hiti III was a master tactician
and a born administrator. He
would surpass his late father,
Chiti II, in both executive manumission
and in forging non-war conquests and
expansion.

After a protracted review of history
and how his ancestors and fathers
moved from a nomadic, migrating, and
raiding tribe to a settlement at Ng'wena,
the emperor and his Council of Chiefs
instituted alliance-making as a new form
of expansion.

"Chief Mwamba reporting. Your
Majesty, I have liaised with the elders
who have had dominating influence
over my great grandfather's Kalundu
Kingdom which my said grandfathers
Mwamba Kashampupo, and Mubanga
Kashampupo as Mwine Tuna Mwamba
II after him, presided over as
Munkonge I, and here, Your Majesty, is
the agreement signifying their consent

to come under your rule."

"Chief Makasa reporting. Your great grandfather, our worshipful Chitimukulu Chilyamafwa, set up the Mpanda Kingdom over which my grandfather, Nondompya who reigned as Makasa I presided. Today, with the blessing of your offer for autonomy, I bring to you an executed agreement of their willingness to submit to your liegeship in perpetuity."

"Thank you, chiefs Mwamba and Makasa for the good news. I want now to hear a report from you, Chief Nkolemfumu, have you resolved the matter of order with subordinate Chief Mpepo?" Emperor Chiti III enquired.

"Indeed, Your Majesty. As you're aware, disputes loom large in our lineage owing to the bifurcation nature of our succession system."

"I know, and I am curious. Last time when my father wanted to amalgamate their line into the chiefdom, they resisted greatly. I remember that my father had decided to leave them hanging. I will not let that happen, especially with all the threats from the remnant of the *Ngonis* and the *foreigners'* looming."

"Your Majesty, they made demands."

"Wha…what? You said demands?"

"Yes, Your Majesty. They want to second Chief Malole's first born daughter, Princess Ruth Mpande, to your service. She will serve you until Your Majesty marries and enthrones a queen."

Breathless with anger, the emperor stood up and walked out, and the retinue sentinel that followed him could sense rage pulsating through his veins.

That millipede of a chief. How dare he does challenge me, Mwine Lubemba *(owner of the Bemba Empire). He wants to hold me on a leash, knowing every secret and decisions I contemplate. Who does he think he is?*

Kabwe Mpaisha, the emperor's assistant, bowed down his head and said, "I wonder if it would help Your Majesty to know that Princess Mpande is considered to be the most beautiful woman in the empire."

The next thing Kabwe saw were the fluffy blossoming eyebrows of the emperor, breezy and sodden, mirroring the emperor's rising mood.

"Is that so?"

"Yes, Your Majesty, except…"

"Except what, Kabwe?"

Kabwe looked left and right as if he was trying to find the right words to use in order not to offend the emperor.

"They say that she is very intoxicated with the *foreigner*'s religion. She prays and attends their meetings more often than most young ladies."

"Oh, really, we will see, let's rejoin everyone inside."

After rejoining the Assembly gathering, the emperor cleared his throat briskly and nodded, giving a sign to Nkolemfumu that he had accepted their demands.

Just when the emperor was about to call for the next report, Nkolemfumu interrupted.

"If I may be allowed to say something further, Your Majesty?"

"Please go on."

"To show commitment and seriousness to this issue, Princess Mpande is *here*, she is waiting outside."

Lamely and disinterestedly, the

emperor beckoned for the princess to be brought in.

The doors suddenly flung open, and first it was as if he was seeing shadows.

Then the shadows cleared and gave way to the darkly shining sun. And as he continued to adjust his eyes, he could barely notice her short moon shadow-black hair and the gothic cotton and wool European-made clothes swiveling to her moving limbs sticking treacherously to her hard two paw-paw ligating backyard as if suspended on a quietly protruding pendulum.

Halfway to the inner circle, she paused as if counting how many *boys* were staring at her oblongly-shaped breasts, exposing all her benevolence and charms, and then she smiled, gracefully thrusting her honey flowing sweet lips.

She was brazening with irresistible joy, steady and relaxed as if palace life had her name on its every door.

She looked up, then sideways before gazing fluently straight at *her* emperor, revealing her cheerful personality.

Her velvety eyelashes, shiny, halo-white teeth, and a burnished complexion, sent chills into the emperor's spine.

All the emperor could say was, "Wow!"

And everyone heard the emperor but dared not utter a single word.

Kabwe was right, what beauty – I have never laid these *eyes of mine on such beauty before,* the emperor forgot that he was presiding over a meeting and went into deep thinking.

To everyone's surprise, Princess Mpepo was directed by the emperor himself to occupy the queen's empty throne that was on his right hand.

The chiefs joked to one another, "Unofficially."

The royal proceedings progressed as normal from then on.

Then in the middle of the proceedings and as if the emperor had been thinking about it ever since he gazed his eyes on Princess Mpepo, he spoke, "Don't Mpepos usually come to rulership through the Nkolemfumu's throne?"

There was hesitation, no-one knew

exactly to whom the question was directed nor the historicity of that issue.

It had started to feel awkward until Princess Mpepo responded, "Yes, Your Majesty, And I should add that both chiefs Mpepo and Nkolemfumu are nominal junior descendants of the Chitimukulu. But tradition has permitted Nkolemfumu to inherit the Mwamba throne. Occasionally, as it was during the case in the Mpande Uprising, His Highness, Chitimukulu Chilyamafwa, wouldn't dare his younger brother, Mubanga Kashampupo, to ascend the *Lubemba* throne when he was still alive, so, he made an exception and required both chiefs Mpepo and Nkolemfumu to go directly to the Chitimukulu throne, although that right was only reserved for the Chitimukulu's senior brothers, Nkula and Mwamba."

The Assembly stood for a resounding ovation.

Some chiefs did not even know whether they had stood because of the speech the princess had made or because of her eloquence.

It was mystifying.

Emperor Chiti III stood up while presiding, for the first time since he inherited the throne from his father.

"I…I am astounded," Emperor Chiti III stammered.

The entire Assembly stood up again and gave another standing ovation to Princess Mpepo.

***

It was clear from that moment onwards that the emperor had become greatly endeared to Princess Mpepo.

From there, there was nowhere the emperor was without Princess Mpepo. The duo took trips to the Kasama and Mpulamasanga lodges frequently.

It became the emperor's habit to be absent from official duties which he conveniently delegated to the Chief's Council under the conservatorship of Chief Mwamba.

CHAPTER 16 | TALES FOR THE AGES

H and in hand, the two newlyweds walked down the long riverbank towards the lake shore, with their assistants keeping a distance.

After the wedding, Princess Mpepo acquired a new royal title of Queen Ruth Mutale. She had resisted removing "Ruth" from her names, "because it preserves my Christian upbringing."

Emperor Chiti III did not mind as long as the queen was happy and retained her role as traditional matriarch of her people.

"*Love*, I have a surprise for you," Emperor Chiti III disclosed to his wife.

"What more can you give me than being your queen and the mother of *Lubemba*?"

"I see. But being a wife is not a gift, I see it as matter of mutual consent."

"Oh, no, hold it right there, my love. You had to break royal protocol and traditions. I was expendable – to be discarded after use. Tradition dictated that you use me as a shooting target to prove your own manhood, then marry a real queen, from a real royal line. Am I lying?"

"Of course, you're, as a matter of custom, telling the truth. But as a matter…"

"Let me finish for you…of heart?"

"You, you, you…" Emperor Chiti tickled his wife on her dimpled bellybutton and the two rolled along with laughter and wrestling on the lake shore sand like two little toddlers.

After returning to Kasama Lodge, where the emperor was first schooled in the intricacies of statehood by his late father and emperor, both Nonde Ng'uni and Kabwe Mpaisha, the respective personal assistants to the queen and the emperor, got busy preparing a banquette to sit four people, the two royals and a mysterious visitor whom the emperor referred to as a "gift." The fourth person was the visitor's associate.

***

The man who showed up took the queen's breath away.

He was probably in his mid-thirties, wearing a well-pressed black suite with a white shirt and a black bow-tie, something very uncommon for a non-aristocratic Black African.

He spoke to his associate, a young Black man of about twenty years, in fluent English: "Take a seat and prepare my cigar."

Queen Ruth Chileshe both heard and noticed.

"And who is this polished gentleman, Love?"

"I will let him speak for himself, Darling."

"I am James Chuma, Sir and Ma'am."

"James – you're a Christian?"

"Yes, Ma'am. I acquired a new name after being baptized by the Rev. John Wilson of Free Church College, in the land called Bombay, in a country known as India, across an endless sea."

"Interestingly!" Queen Mutale was flabbergasted.

"He is *the* gift I told you about, I can see you are liking it," Emperor Chiti III teased his wife.

The new visitor did not wait for the queen to ask another question; he could read her mind.

"I am originally a Wayaus from Nyasa, sold as a slave and rescued by my late master, David Livingstone, may his soul rest in peace."

"Darling, this man is the only African from these lands who has ever stepped a foot into the *foreigners'* land, and he came back," the emperor explained.

"Really, amazing, tell me, did you see in their country, where they print Bibles?" The queen directed her question to James.

"Not only where they print Bibles, but also other books on science, religion, history, law and the like. I assisted in the publication of my late master's manuscript. They are well advanced ahead of us, Ma'am."

When he finished speaking, James Chuma motioned to his associate to bring for him a box containing pipes of bange. Chuma got into his pouch and removed a lighter and after lighting one cigar, he began to smoke.

I have seen it with Father Dixon. They called it tobacco. He smoked it without stopping making that crazy noise – moto-moto-moto, hence, they called him, 'Father Motomoto!'

The queen thought and then laughed.

"Something delightful, Darling?"

"James reminds me of Father Dixon with that tobacco of his."

"What is a tobacco?" Emperor Chiti III asked.

"*That thing*," Queen Chileshe pointed to the pipe James Chuma was smoking.

"You want to try?" James Chuma offered the royals.

"Not me," Queen Chileshe politely declined.

"I will try it," Emperor Chiti III accepted.

"But as per security protocol, Kabwe will try it first," the emperor regulated.

When the emperor's personal assistant pushed one, two and three, he coughed incessantly and then he began to laugh.

After taking ten puffs, his eyes were red hot and fluidy.

He became buoyant and lackadaisical.

"He over did it. First time, take a little, and little and then more," James Chuma advised.

The emperor did not have a coughing experience, but he became overtly excited, a feeling that he described as, "awesome!"

"*James*, tell me more about your expeditions and experience with David and England?" Queen Chileshe wanted to know.

"My Livingstone died few years ago. I and my childhood friend, Susi, ferried him across gigantic oceans to England. We met his son and daughter and visited many interesting places and ate 'bread' and drank 'dry gin.'"

James paused, and then he continued.

"Before he died, his baggage with medicine case containing *quinin* was stolen. We managed to brave the bugs around Lake Bangueulu and finally reached Chief Chitambo's village carrying him on a *kitanda*. There, at night, he died while uttering prayers to God the Father."

"Wait right there, he died praying?" Queen Ruth Chileshe exclaimed with excitement.

"Yes, I personally left him praying, after Majwara and Susi gave him the last of the pills we had salvaged, and in the morning, a female helper found him dead, kneeling in the same posture we were told."

"Incredible!" The queen was excited.

"But…" James began.

"But what?" Queen Chileshe asked.

"It was not *me* who saw him kneeling contrary to what the *papers* reported in England."

"Why would they do that?" Queen Chileshe probed.

"I really don't know, but I can speculate."

"Hmh?" Queen Chileshe aided James.

"Yes, Ma'am, I think that they wanted the English populous to believe that God was pleased with the Doctor."

The emperor was not interested in

that aspect of conversation. He
motioned to his queen not to follow up
with another question.

"James, ignore my wife's
interceptions, between me and your
God, she loves him more, I know,"
Emperor Chiti III who was now high
on *bange* persuaded James Chuma to
continue.

"Sure, Your Majesty. Some Christian
medical personnel in our caravan
carried out an autopsy and we buried
his heart in a tin box under a *mvula tree*
right there at Chitambo's village. Chief
Chitambo was generous to us."

"Mhm, then?" Emperor Chiti III
prodded James on.

"But his body was buried with
honors in England. They gave me *these*."

James Chuma showed them two
plaques, a Royal Geographical Society
medal, a silver medal, and a sword.

The royals inspected the plaques and
the sword, with great admiration.

"Should I add?" James Chuma asked.

"Please, sure, continue," Queen
Chileshe invited.

"My poor Livingstone was doubted

and feared dead until Henry Morton presumed it was Livingstone and proved the Society otherwise. And it is remarkable that poor Bishop MacKenzie also died in similar circumstances like Livingstone. They both ran out of their meds. Other versions state that their meds were stolen. This begs me to assert…"

"Assert what?" Emperor Chiti III prompted.

"Your Majesty, that with good medicines, the empire's lives can be elongated. If His Majesty wants to build a lasting empire, he should invest in good medicines."

"And how do I do that?"

"Invite scientists and doctors to your empire. Give them power to conduct research and produce their findings. You will be amazed what our local trees can produce, Your Majesty."

"Yes, this is what I have been trying to tell him!" Queen Chileshe exclaimed.

"You two planned this – *Kabwe*, look at these two connivers," the emperor joked.

"May I speak?" Kabwe asked.

"Go ahead," Emperor Chiti III gave Kabwe permission.

"His Majesty is afraid that when he gives them one inch, they would take over his empire."

Queen Chileshe reacted with extemporaneity.

"Stop that nonsense, Kabwe. I grew up under Christian influence. And look at James, he went to England, and did they kill him? No. They brought him back and now he is an asset to all of us – teaching science and communication."

"Apparently, Kabwe is right. But I want to hear James' wisdom, please continue, James," the emperor said.

"I am sure His Majesty is aware that his father, Emperor Chiti II, ended slavery in Bembaland. That was the fight of Livingstone until he died. As I indicated, I was a slave, and it was he who rescued me. Indeed, *these* are good people. Currently, I work under Bishop Thomson of Universities' Mission to Central Africa near these areas. And my wife, Ntaoéka, is currently head of women health and reproduction."

"What does she do as head of health and reproduction?" Queen Chileshe asked.

"She teaches women the importance of good health and of spacing children to prevent overpopulation."

"May I speak?" Nonde Ng'uni, the queen's personal assistant asked.

"Indeed, yes, go ahead, Nonde," Queen Chileshe did not object.

"Why teach women to space children, wouldn't that depopulate the land? And maybe even cause warrior shortages."

"I like that line of thinking, Nonde," Emperor Chiti III approved.

"*Nonde, don't talk again*," Queen Chileshe did not agree with her own assistant.

"Yes, Your Highness," Nonde responded, penitently.

"I have two concerns, though, Your Majesty, and this was the reason why I wanted to see you urgently."

"What are they, James?" Asked the emperor.

CHAPTER 17 | SPIRITS LAUGH

Emperor Chiti III adjusted his sitting position on a wooded highchair. He was keen on hearing what James Chuma would say.

"I am all ears, James."

"First, I have *this* letter, it has been with me for more than ten years," James Chuma handed over the letter to Kabwe to give it to the emperor.

Kabwe was directed by the emperor through a shoulder gesture to forward it to Queen Chileshe who was proficient in English.

The queen started to read the letter:

From: British Colonial Office
To: Charles MacKenzie, UMCA
Date: July 1862

Your grace is wished an expedited recovery from malaria. His grace would be reminded to take quinin as frequently in order to offset fever and debilitating aches.

Within thirty or less days the *Pioneer*, revamped and repaired with the British taxpayers' money, will arrive. It has been refurbished with a new wooden paddle survey vessel. Your request has, thus, been extended.

The Colonial Office reminds his grace to commission both David Livingstone and Horace Waller who are presently in Central Africa to use the ploy of ending slavery as a bait in order to convince many leading chiefs to surrender their land to the British government.

Tactics used elsewhere, such as in India, have proved that if you offer concessions or promise to develop these lands, at Her Majesty the Queen's expense, they will bulge and give in. But the most efficient and cost-effective method of colonization is through the proselytization of the infidels.

Target very powerful kings and chiefs. Once the mission stations are established, root the people into our culture and way of life. That way, it would be easier for Her Majesty to lay claim to the mineral wealth and soil rich Africa.

The Colonial Office has

acquiesced to your revised budget which will be reflected in the next payment to the UMCA and to your personal account.

Yours,
Colonial Office, UK.

"Your concerns are reasonable, James. I was aware of the *foreigners'* machinations through my father when he brought me here and lectured me. Ever since, I have been suspicious of them."

"But do you have the response from the missions to this letter?" Queen Chileshe wanted to know.

"No. As you can see, this letter was written when I was barely twelve or so years. There definitely could have been a response I am not aware of."

"You don't need to have been aware of anything, James. Everything you need to know is in this letter. The Government of England funds the missions and uses them to eventually grab our land, our way of life. Our sages say, *Lufwinyemba aliwa pa kantu* or a problem child is known to repeat the same mistakes, implying that, 'investigate and you will find the truth.'")

169

"Thanks, Your Majesty. And to you, *Ma'am*, I should add, when I was in England, a child followed me and told me to shower so that I could become like them, *white*. I think that His Majesty is correct, no matter what we do, they will always think that we don't measure up."

"But James, don't listen to His Majesty; he's biased."

"Darling, no matter how hard you polish iron, it would not turn into gold, and vice versa. We must be who we are, and if we deal with the *foreigners*, it must be at our terms or with mutual respect and consideration. That's all I want for my people."

"Your Highness, unfortunately, His Majesty is correct," James stated, with a sense of seriousness in his tone, for the first time since he began conversing with the royals.

"Tell me your second concern, James."

"It's the Mazitu, Your Majesty."

"Who is Mazitu?"

"It's the Ngunis, Darling. Go ahead, *James*."

"Their raids have just worsened, Your Majesty. What are you going to do about that?"

"Thank you for your concern, James. It's also my concern. Once they boasted that us the *baBembas* were thieves because we raided for survival. But now they are desperate. Next time we meet, James, this problem would have disappeared."

"I am assured, Your Majesty."

The royals were tired and wanted to retire to bed.

"See you, James, hope we meet again."

"Goodbye, Your Majesty, Your Highness."

***

Before he left, a sudden burst of whirlwind blew from northeast bringing a mixture of chills and warm surges, not only in the nearby forest but in the hills and gorges surrounding James' soul.

He almost fell to the ground, albeit without attracting attention to the people around him. He shivered momentarily and then regained his composure.

A pyrrhic thought hit his heart, bumping him into internal turbulence.

He felt like he was dying.

It was an experience he had been having ever since he traveled through that ocean he called "Hellway." He couldn't keep it to himself anymore, or it might stop his heart.

He summoned all the strength and eloquence he had left after a protracted discussion with the royals, and then he asked.

"Excuse me, Your Majesty. If it pleases His Royaliness, that I may have a brief talk with him – privately."

"Of course," Emperor Chiti III gestured with his right hand that everyone should leave them alone.

They all left.

"Do you know the meaning of the word 'hypocrisy,' Your Majesty?"

"It…"

"No need to, Your Majesty, I meant it as a rhetorical question. My Livingstone might have been a devoted Christian, and I respect that, but…"

"But what, James?" Emperor Chiti III hugged James around the shoulders, literally, balancing him as he stumbled headlong.

"James, is everything alright?"

"No, Your Majesty. You have to see to believe what I saw. These people, so-called *Europeans* or even *foreigners*, whatever you may call them, are pure hypocrites. Those boats you see dock around here, are simply decoys. They stop at numerous harbors throughout their journey to their land, and Your Majesty, it is a travesty – they load smaller ships with an insurmountable number of our people, our kind, and pack them like your small *inkisakisa* (small fishes), with no clean water or food – eating each other's fingers on a rotational basis, and swimming *mumafi* (faeces) and *imisu* (urine) of one another. It is pathetic, Your Majesty."

"Hey, stop right there, James, what are you saying? You mean…" Emperor Chiti III made nonverbal gestures suggesting that *foreigners* themselves transport African slaves across the sea.

"Yes. And even worse as I have stated. When I arrived in England, I saw for myself the remnants of our 'Black people,' as they call them, the haciendas they had built, and the plantations and almost all of England is saturated with slave labor."

"James, this is disturbing. You mean our

people are the ones who are developing *their* land?"

"You can say that, and more. So-called Black people are forced to change their culture; they don't even remember their ancestral names anymore. I am lucky I served 'Chuma' in my name; for those who slave it in England, they lost all connections to 'Africa,' as they call our land. Some are called Johnson Jackson or Ben Kelly or any other combination of the European names."

"What you're saying, James, is that *they* are here to annihilate our personality, culture and history?"

"Yes, Your Majesty. If we do nothing, our authentic kingdoms like yours will be only an appendage of history. And…"

"And what, Chuma, let me call you 'Chuma' after what you've just told me?"

"Your Majesty, family, the notion of family doesn't exist any more among those who used to be our people. They are no longer people, but properties of these *foreigners*. I have never seen a kind of people who are heartless, not even to consider a tiny bit of humanity in Africans. They consider them 'things' and even less than dogs and cats – which are accommodated more decently than the Black-African slaves. They are also immoral, far from the sermons my Livingstone used to preach. In one situation, I saw people who are called 'Coloreds' and these were born from insipid actions. A master, as they call slave owners, would simply rape the Black-African women in full view of their husbands, Your Majesty."

At this moment, Chuma ran out of words, and he began to sob.

Emperor Chiti III gave him balance and asked Nonde to bring some water for Chuma.

As Nonde was about to leave, the emperor stopped her.

"*Nonde*, I want you to hear what Chuma is saying. I saw that you care for these issues."

Chuma continued after a brief respite and what he said next confirmed the emperor's fears.

"Thank you, Your Majesty. These people have three characteristics. They come like sheep, but they are wolves. They show fake sympathy, but their end is to erase all of what we are and what we know.

And they can say 'sorry,' but they don't mean it – for example, in their land, they've passed laws to end slavery, but those who are so freed are subjected to worse economic and social conditions than even those who are still in bondage. Some *journalists*, as they call those who write for public readership in what they call *newspapers*, even wrote about me when I arrived – see this (Chuma shows the emperor a newspaper cutting from the *Morning Herald*). They called me 'baboon,' 'uncivilized,' 'landless vagabond,' and as 'Livingstone's slave.' What troubled me the most *there* was the fact that my Livingstone used to tell me that I was not his slave – but all that England knew was that I was, in fact, his slave. Can you imagine, Your Majesty? So, when they are with us, they tell us lies, the only thing that matters to them is to grab us, as their property and to, eventually, Your Majesty, come and take our land, Africa."

The emperor paused for a long time without saying a word.

The revelation had stung the royal like a bite of a wasp. All that his father had told him was true.

I wonder what Dad would say if he heard this, the emperor thought.

Then he thought about James Chuma personally and how he must have been confused, so confused that despite having that firsthand knowledge, he was still hopeless and found himself working for the missionaries.

It's like flying straight from the pan into the fire; he's rescued from slavery only to be delivery to another form of slavery, only more dispiriting, he thought.

The emperor's stupor was only cut short by Nonde's interjection.

"I have been very suspicious. No-one leaves such far lands and go through impassable voyages just to come and part us on our backs, Majesty."

The emperor invoked his father's memory as he agreed with Nonde.

"Dad was right, Nonde. He had long known that there was something wrong with these *foreigners*."

"What shall we do, Majesty?" Nonde asked.

"I will table this before the Chiefs' Council for debate."

"Majesty, does this require debate?"

As if he had forgotten something vey important, James Chuma interrupted the emperor and Nonde's conversation and said, "Before you can deal with issues of debate, Your Majesty, I have one more thing."

The emperor turned towards James, leaving Nonde waiting and in a lurch, and said, "Go ahead, Chuma."

"Your Majesty, I know that you're a proud Miti Clan?"

"Indeed, I am."

"Do you know what will happen to *Lubemba* if you allow the *foreigners* to take over your land?"

"I can only guess."

"The trees will be cut, and they will be unhappy. In London, all the accoutrements of nature are hardly in existence. Concrete and artificial loans have replaced the natural green world as we know it here – as God intended us to take care of the earth."

"What do they think?"

"I think they think that it looks beautiful and civilized. But I differ. I think that it destroys nature, and in the end, there will be poor air and all sorts of bad elements rubbing shoulders with humans."

"I agree with you, Chuma."

***

A stream flowed astride Kasama Lodge. It was clear, greenish like the trees that lined along its overcast banks silhouetted through the perfect warm evening sheds, giving the impression that heaven and earth had kissed.

The sky fell dancingly across the horizon, bringing a feeling of harmony and peace to the fading sunset.

The waters were clear, the earth ready, and the sky eager.

As he walked lazily, counting the leaves as they waved good night to what had been one of the calmest afternoons around Kasama Lodge, his eyes fell nonchalantly onto a figure emerging from wading waters, swimming innocently like a virgin goddess mermaid.

He barely recognized her.

Elegant.

Beautiful.

And naked.

"*Kabwe*, I want you to bring Nonde into my chambers tonight."

"Yes, Your Majesty."

***

"Kunda, Kunda!" Nonde called out.

"I am here, Ma'am, Madam Tendai."

"Don't refer to me as *Ma'am* from now onwards. I carry an emperor in my belly," Nonde expressed her excitement while directing Kunda's hands towards her still flat tummy.

"You don't need to do this…*Ma'am*, I mean, Nonde."

The two laughed as they conversed with one another.

"But on a serious note, what does all this mean?" Kunda Lumbwe wanted to know.

"The *plan* is in motion, Mwisange, I mean Kunda. When *this* starts to show, I want you to admit that you're the father of the child. Don't forget why we came here, do you?"

"Yes, Nonde. But what about the other promise you made, my beloved 'Morning Staress'?"

"I'm aware. I have talked to Ruth already; you'll definitely be Sampa's chief bodyguard very soon."

"Thank you, *Ma'am*, I mean, Nonde."

CHAPTER 18 | WOLVES DANCE

Complex and intelligent. Wolves are complex, highly intelligent animals who are caring, playful, and above all devoted to family.

Only a select few other species exhibit these traits so clearly. Just like elephants, gorillas and dolphins, wolves educate their young, take care of their injured and live in family groups.

The wolf has developed the capacity to survive in the most inhospitable of climates. The wolves in the high arctic endure several winter months. Other wolves are at home in the desert and the dampness of a humid Gulf Coast swamp.

Wolf rank order within a pack is established and maintained through a series of 'ritualized fights' and posturing best described as 'ritual bluffing.'

Wolves prefer psychological warfare to physical confrontations, meaning that high-ranking status is based more on personality or attitude than on size or physical strength.

***

It would be over seven years since Emperor Chiti Chitapankwa (Chiti III) had been sitting on his throne without the shadow of his father hanging over his shoulders. Six elevated semi-thrones were erected only lower than the emperor's own. Seated on the six thrones were chiefs Nkula, Mwamba, Nkole, Makasa, Chikwanda, and Commander General Mporokoso. They were adorned in black and white gowns embroidered in greenish forest-shaped ornaments. The emperor himself was lightly adorned, wearing a foreign made shirt and a hat made from crocodile skin.

He has had a hold on his empire owing to his orderly administration and total control of the affairs of the peripheral chieftainships. Outside the palace throne room were lined up missionaries, explorers, traders, skilled professionals, and the commoners seeking for the emperor's wisdom and counsel.

He was the first emperor to encourage his people to ask him questions on the state of the empire. He was never opprobrious but generous and his people found in him to be like a father figure who was genuinely concerned about his people's welfare.

The emperor announced agenda items for the day which included the Nguni raids on the outskirts of the Bemba Empire which were threatening to weaken the empire.

Some sub-chiefs in remote areas of the empire were constantly being enticed by foreigners and traders to start Susula-like revolts.

Some sub-chiefs were conducting dubious long-distance trade directly with the Arabs and the Swahili traders in violation of the *Maluba Reform* protocols.

"Your Majesty, all of these issues except one are related," Chief Makasa observes.

"I agree with Chief Makasa. All the other issues have to do with foreigners. Only the raids deal with security. I think that it is a common problem that expansion brings. When the empire is too large, it may be too hard to monitor activities taking place on the far outskirts," Chief Chikwanda advises.

"So, what do we do, counsellors?"

Emperor Chiti III asks the chiefs.

"For the problem of raids, I suggest that we decentralize security. Indeed, my office is situated in Ng'wena, but I depend on the messages reported to me by the *Kapaso* and warrior messenger. These may take a long time before I am aware of the problem. We can give the chiefs power to create local enforcers who report to the chiefs and the chiefs report to us. I suggest we give each chief here a jurisdiction of, say, one hundred sub-chiefs who report to them, and once they compile their reports, they can brief Your Majesty."

"I concur with Chief Mporokoso," Nkole agreed.

After a short debate, all the six chiefs came to a unanimous agreement that Chief Mporokoso's suggestion was proper, with some modifications.

"With regards to trade, Your Majesty, I suggest that we form alliances with the missionaries and trade liaisons in each locale. That way, we will hold these organizations accountable if they thwart trade rules and guidelines. This will send fear into everyone who wants to dupe our trade arrangements," Chief Mwamba suggested.

"I am with Chief Mwamba, Your Majesty, but in addition, we must provide an incentive to the missionaries and traders so that they find trading with the central government more convenient and more rewarding than with thugs," Chief Nkula refined Chief Mwamba's suggestion.

As with Chief Mporokoso's suggestion, everyone largely agreed with Chief Mwamba's suggestion, with modifications. Emperor Chiti III set up two task forces, one headed by Chief Mporokoso and the other one by Chief Mwamba to finalize the leaders' decision regarding security and trade, respectively.

***

"I suggest, Darling, that we do both, as my father used to say as he learned from Father Ignatius, that we give to Caesar what is Caesar's and to God what is God's. That way, our people will be contented with their ancestral traditions and our missionary partners will be pacified."

Emperor Chiti III's wife, *Lute* (Ruth) Mutale, first-born daughter of Chief Malole of Malole's village, was a devout Christian who was schooled in the intricacies of foreign numeracy and languages. She knew at least two foreign languages, *Icisungu* (English) and *Icilatini* (Latin).

She was seconded to the empire following the *Mwamba Reforms* which prescribed an exchange of protection and guns to the empire for a Christian wife for the emperor. The reforms targeted St. Francis Mission, the largest missionary conclave in and near Bembaland for secondment. Chief Malole was believed to have been a direct descendant of Chama Kampamba, believed to have been the young sister of Mukulumpe from the Luba Kingdom. As such, Lute Mutale was considered to be a rightful queen to produce a legitimate heir to the Bemba Empire.

"I had accepted a traditional, customary marriage, compromising my Christian upbring and beliefs. It's your turn now to give in to your traditional, cultural beliefs and accept that we dedicate our baby according to God's holy word."

"Okay, fine, Darling, what if we meet each other halfway – we dedicate him to a

Christian God, but I choose to give him a name?"

The suggestion made by the emperor pleased Queen Ruth Mutale and the church, and the son was dedicated to the Christian God.

***

"*Your Majesty*, Queen Mutale is outside the door; she would like to see you," Kabwe informed the emperor.

"She may wait, Kabwe, I have urgent matters now."

"Your Majesty, you know how persistent the queen is. Last time when I delayed her, she sent bees to my cottage."

"Kabwe…I-I-I…you…"

The queen stormed into the chamber and asked everyone to leave them alone.

"You forget that I am your *wife* and I…I have certain needs?"

"Come on, Darling, I…I am reviewing a document, a contract *your* mission would like me to consider."

The queen calmed down.

She had a notable weakness for church affairs.

"Oh…sorry, Love, I didn't know that you were doing something important. So, what is it all about?"

"It's nothing. St. Francis Mission is recommending that I subject my reign to a sort of a *company* in exchange for more protection and a thirty percent per annum kind of profit sharing. As you know, my English isn't very good yet. I was trying to understand the document with the help of the Records Office personnel."

"My English is good, and so are my libido tonight…"

"Hmm…do you mean, you will translate these for me after…"

"So long as we are not *creating* another Sampa…you know how I hate getting pregnant!"

"Kabwe!"

"Yes, Your Majesty."

"Close the door. No-one enters for the next thirty minutes."

"No, Kabwe, not thirty, but one hour thirty!"

"Yes, Ma'am!"

CHAPTER 19 | MOTIVES ASUNDER

"They just want to help, that's all, Love. If you give them the entirety of Mambweland, they will help develop it and improve transportation. Isn't that what you want?"

"No…I mean, yes, that's what I want, and I don't want. *Lute*, these are dangerous tactics. They didn't come all the way just to be nice to us; they are here to dominate, to take over from us."

"You're wrong, Love."

"I insist, it's dangerous, Darling."

"I don't think so, my love. These are good people, family people."

"I don't doubt that. It's the reason my father and I allowed them to settle in our land."

"So, why do you hate them now, why do you doubt them?"

"No, Darling. It's not them I am attacking."

"They want the same things for us as they do for their families. And if you're not attacking them, what are you attacking?"

"Their behavior, Darling, not who they are, that's what is wrong."

"They preach love and mercy. The Bible supports them, 'You shall know them by their fruits.'"

"Indeed, Darling. But remember that most fruits are not known until they are ripe!"

"You're merciless!"

"Don't forget, Darling, too, that mercy is reasonable, or else…"

"Or else what?"

"You become *Mercy*'s food for lunch like a partridge was!"

"I am not joking, my love."

"Me, either."

"But at least sign that contract to show commitment, hmm, my husband."

"What do you mean by signing a 'contract'?"

"That document you have is called a contract. When you sign or affix your thumb on those dotted lines, it means that you can't change your mind later; so, will they, they must keep their promise."

"Is that true?"

"Of course, yes."

"Darling, don't think that sometimes I don't …"

"Don't do what?"

"That I don't care about us – you and Sampa and your God."

"I know you care for me and our child, I just don't think that you regard my God and brethren that high."

"No, that's not true, in fact, I should be grateful."

"What do you mean you should be grateful?"

"Darling, if I told you that I am *Yesu*'s product, can you believe me?"

"Oh…whoa…you want to blaspheme my Savior!"

"No, I want to praise him, you don't understand. My father told me that my mother was barren, and *Yesu* made her have me. I am a miracle child."

"Oh, really, my love, tell me more, why did you keep such nice news from me?" Queen Ruth Mutale joyous. She came closest to him and held him tightly around the abdomen, kissing his hairless head.

"*Yesu* is good, very good. But some people try to dominate others in his name. Those are the people whose behavior I

191

hate. As emperor, you must always distinguish between genuine believers and imposters, otherwise you may wake up one day without a realm."

"I love you even more, Darling."

"Does that mean who will support me against these imposters?"

"Yes, but if you first fix me good, *Lute*!"

"I will *kill* you!"

"Oh, Darling. I-I am already dead, you can't *kill* dead."

"Alright, here I come…"

***

During the following meeting in the Council of Chiefs, Emperor Chiti III tabled the demands of the company from the south that wanted land and mineral prospecting in Bembaland. The emperor went at length to explain the contents of the document called "contract" which his wife, the queen, had taken trouble to explain to him from page to page.

"Your Majesty, you're a wise ruler. You did well not to accept the terms or sign on the dotted lines before discussing it with us," began Senior Chief Mwamba Mulenga

Chipoya.

"A slave who recently ran away from King Lewanika told me that this same company forced the king to sign the same documents, and now he has no control over the land."

"I knew it!" Emperor Chiti III exclaimed.

Then the emperor recalled how his late father had warned him of the foreigners. He had told him to be cautious and not to give away his birth right.

"These foreigners don't mean well to us; they are wealth hunters," he remembered his father alerting him.

"But I fear that the queen may influence you to sign that document, Your Majesty. Forgive me."

Chief Nkula was bold to direct his comment at the emperor.

"It pleases me that we are having this debate. As you know I trust this Council and your wisdom is invaluable to me," declared the emperor.

"I do have a suggestion, Your Majesty," Chief Nkole stated.

"We are all ears." Emperor Chiti III replied.

"That document, Your Majesty, and respectable friends, is our doorway to development. How about we make a copy of it and give back the original to the company."

"Then what do we do with the duplicable?" Chief Makasa asked.

"We carry out all the suggested projects mentioned in it. We can easily do that with the profit from trading with the Arabs and the Swahili, isn't it so Chief Mporokoso?"

"In other words, the company has brought us ideas right within our laps?" Chief Mwamba connected the dots.

"That's right. And more…" Chief Nkole invoked.

"What more?" Chief Mwamba wanted to know.

"We begin mining activities for gold and copper in the areas they asked for. How else would they ask for those areas if they saw nothing valuable in them?"

The Chief's Council's deliberations pleased the emperor, and he constructed a three-member taskforce to look into the issue of developing the indicated areas for gold, silver, and copper. The *Nkole-Nkula-Mwamba Taskforce* would be headed by

Chief Nkole and would undertake investigations and research and make recommendations to the Council within twelve months. It would also canvass the help of the Arabs in the acquisition of the equipment and instruments suggested by the company in the unsigned contract.

The emperor ended the meeting with, "It is decreed."

***

When Queen Ruth Chileshe heard what the Council had decided she was enraged. She was worried that the mission would construe the refusal as an afront and it might demote her father from priesthood and deregister their son and heir to throne, Chiti Sampa, from catechism.

But she was frustrated by something else; politics only worsened her emotions. Her Christian profession clashed with her husband's desire to preserve the traditions and customs of his ancestors.

She remembered how she was already thinking of divorcing him because of his strict adherence to traditional rituals, observations and rites regarding childbirth, and personal hygiene and libido. She felt sexually starved when she became pregnant with her son and heir to the throne, Sampa. Her husband wouldn't dare even to touch her body because of fear of offending *imipashi*.

"*Mutale Chitapankwa Muluba*!"

She called him out by his own name and then she expressed her frustration.

"You know a woman's nature, before and after the catamenial cycle, she needs attention. I need that!"

He casually parted her on her right thigh, winked from the side of his left eye and comforted her.

"But you're *the* queen of a very powerful empire, you have to make sacrifices, Darling."

She pumped up in blushing and anger as if to tell him that it mattered most to her. He stood up, followed her as she sat hard on a foam made mattress, the two only such in the entire empire. Hers was traded with an Arab entrepreneur in exchange for four pieces of gold. The other one belonged to Bishop Charles Shaw of the Central Africa Mission Society (CAM) under the LMS stationed at Ulala Mission near Chitambo village in the Kingdom of Kazembe.

Bishop Shaw was, at that time, in the process of setting up three residential mission stations at Kawimbe, Kambole, Mpolokoso, and one at Mbereshi where missionaries would set up a quinine clinic in honor of Dr. David Livingstone whose heart remained buried under a tree few kilometers from there.

"Look, look at the front door, all my doing?"

"What are you talking about, you mean those two breasts and *impande* shells…that is simply your…"

"Yes, my weapons? No…those are for your pleasure, my Lord…but…"

"But what?"

"You neglect me, I mean you are not always here, at least in your mind."

"What matters, Darling, is that I love you…but each time we do it, you refuse to purify yourself after the act, I mean, to perform a purifying ritual of washing. It infuriates *imipashi*."

There was a knock on their bedroom door.

Sampa's voice echoed through the halls.

"Dad, Mom."

"Hmm…is there a problem, Son?" His mother asks.

"No, Mom. Kabwe is in the waiting room; he wants to see Father."

His father, who had heard the conversation, nodded, and he nearly stumbled while putting on his royal robe. He heard his son's gently tapping on his inner chamber's door.

It must be something very important, the emperor thought.

He came outside to get on the chariot.

"General Mporokoso sent word, Your Majesty," Kabwe reported, in a panting voice, sufficient enough to be heard by the queen.

"I think they have decided."

His wife, the queen heard him. From inside the palace lounge she shouted.

"Love, what you have decided will place a wedge between you and the church," Queen Chileshe confronts her husband, walking daringly past him, stopping him just before he put his right leg on the chariot's axle.

The emperor orders the retinue to leave them alone.

"Leave us everyone."

They all left.

"Why is the Church interested in the work of the company, Darling?"

"Be…cause, well, I don't know. I just feel that you will not be fulfilling the purpose of the reason why you married me."

"Well, let me tell you. I might have at first married you because of the arrangement. But after living with you for fifteen years, I have come to only one conclusion."

"And which is?"

"That even if there was no arrangement, if there were a million women in Bembaland, or you were the only woman in the world, I would still marry you."

The queen nearly stumbled. She regained her composure and spoke in a low, loving tone.

"Oh, that's so sweet, Love."

Knowing that he had gotten her in the place he wanted her to be. He offered to return sooner. He walked towards her, drew her closest to his chest so she could hear his heartbeat, and he whispered.

"I swear, it'll be pushups when I return

tonight!"

She blushed, shyly.

***

Early the next morning, the well-rested queen pinched her husband to wake up.

"Hmm…I…I am sleepy, Darling."

"I just have one question. What you said last night, did you mean it?"

"I swear on Sampa's life; I meant every one of those words."

"I love you so much, Love."

"Me, too, Darling."

Emperor Chiti III pretended as if he had returned to a deep sleep with heavy snoring.

Meanwhile, he smiled to himself and thought, *Conquering the heart of a woman seems to be tougher than repelling the mindset of foreign interests. Something is telling me that they first want to steal our hearts, and then our land!*

CHAPTER 20 | THE *PLAN*

"Are you really sure you will make this land a Christian nation? That has been my dream. If you could do that, I promise you, I will divorce him and marry you," Queen Ruth Chileshe assured her secret lover, who just happened to be one of the emperor's most trusted insiders.

Their relationship had been platonic, vacillating from promises of divorcing their spouses to insinuations of bringing the empire under the real faith – the Christian faith.

Chief Makasa was a vibrant mid-aged man of exceptional talents and gravitas. He was preternatural and remorseless, icy, and heartless but it was his intriguing and restless character that won the heart of the reigning queen. His fluency with words and the ability to squeeze one at his victim's most vulnerable moments, made it all even easier to dissuade the queen not only to fall for him, but also to join him in the plot to bring the emperor down.

"You dazzled me the first time you appeared in the Assembly. I said to myself, '*Whoa, is this the heavenly goddess herself who has visited her children on earth?*' Oh, Babe, you're simply in the class of your own."

But his lover, the queen, was not your average guileless, devoted wife and mother. She had come to the throne with a plan and mind of her own. Not even her faithful and caring husband, the emperor, could prevent her from achieving it.

She had almost changed her mind after the recent confession by her husband that he loved her for her, and not because of the empire.

But I have reached a place of no return, she thought.

Her relationship with Chief Makasa was sometimes platonic and even plastic. She enjoyed making love with him in secret, but she wanted him to do the one thing that her heartbeat gonged for – converting every soul in *Lubemba* to Christianity.

And having spent close to twenty years with Emperor Chiti III, she knew he was unrelenting, impetuous, and committed to fulfilling his ancestors' dream – to expand

Lubemba beyond the horizons infecting and infesting any challenge with authentic cultural and traditional norms bequeathed to him by his ancestors. She knew that he would not bulge to aligning his interests with those of the Christians although he personally had great respect for the person of the Lord Jesus Christ whom he claimed, "Brought me into this world."

"Are you still dazzled even now that I am carrying your baby, hmm, 'Kasa, hmm?"

"Wha…wha…what are you talking about?" Chief Makasa romps and then it hits him. "How is it possible, you're a married woman, that could as well be his baby?"

Queen Mutale, simultaneously and even unconsciously, vaulted herself tightly to her lover, and making sure that her grooves fit perfectly into his ridges.

She was directly facing his back.

They were both in bed.

They were both naked.

She then, without looking back, directed her hand towards his manhood, held and squeezed it, and said, "This…this is the only *alien* that has been penetrating my orifice in the last four months. Your emperor has been busy ingratiating *spirits* during all that time, you think it's serendipitous?"

"But…"

"But what?"

"Babe, at least you should have told me…that he was not making love to you these last few months."

"Come on, 'Kasa, do you think that if he was making love to me, I would have been sleeping with you?"

"Alright, I get it, you made love to me because he was nowhere to be found…"

"Of course, but now this only complicates things."

"No, on second thoughts, this gives us the opportunity to finish what we started. In less than two hours both Kabwe and Besa will be here, and we should…"

"Do what, 'Kasa, kill them?"

"Not them, him?"

"You mean…?"

"Yes, who else can complete this task seamlessly other than his own personal assistant and his personal physician!"

"I see. You're a clever man, 'Kasa."

"I have a suggestion, Babe, it could

relieve us of collateral damage."

"What is it?"

"Terminate the pregnancy."

"That, I can't do, 'Kasa."

"But why, women do that all the time!"

"I am not just any other woman; I am a Christian."

"So, what, if you are a Christian, wouldn't it bring dishonor to the faith if they find out that you got a child out of wedlock?"

"That's a lesser sin than killing a small child, besides, I'm a married woman, 'Kasa."

"But just a minute a go you agreed to having us, I mean Kabwe and Mungole, kill your husband, what has changed?"

"Nothing, nothing has changed. It's only that…"

"Only what, Babe?" Chief Makasa now faces his lover and wipes out the tears dripping from her eyes.

"A baby is innocent."

"But, Babe, the emperor also can be said to be innocent…"

"No!"

Queen Ruth Mutale stomped out of the bed, grabbed a *chitenge* wrapper and left

Chief Makasa alone, who wondered what she was thinking. In her deep thoughts she was contemplating about the impudence of her husband and the innocence of her unborn child.

He is not innocent. Killing him is doing God's justice. He has resisted the Gospel and held on to sinful practices and traditions. He worships Beelzebub; he deserves to die. But the child is innocent.

Chief Makasa followed her to the other room. He hugged her and wiped her tears again.

They caressed and made love.

They were in the loving-making cooling mood when there was a knock on the door. Kabwe Mpaisha and Besa Mungole were punctual.

Kabwe and Besa had taken advantage of their boss's absence. It was the time when seers went to the royal ancestral shrine to placate the ancestors for good harvest.

Emperor Chiti III had designated himself as *Lubemba*'s General Seer after Seer Chikunga, who had succeeded the Great 'White' Seer, Luchele Ng'anga, had been relieved of his duties. The emperor had journeyed to the shrine accompanied by Shimwalule as per custom.

"You're here, thank God, you came," Queen Rule Chileshe welcomed the two.

"Let us go straight to business as our absence at the palace might alert the guards," Kabwe suggested.

The four deliberated for almost an hour. Kabwe and Mungole were now holding hands openly as a couple would, albeit inside a well-guarded room at a secret resort in Chief Makasa's chiefdom.

It was because of their relationship that they found themselves in that predicament.

Queen Ruth Chileshe had visited her husband at his cottage's study room and unexpectedly she had found the duo making romantic gestures when the emperor was napping.

They had begged her not to tell the emperor because same-sex relationships were unheard of in *Lubemba*. The likely punishment would be castration before burning for men and de-breasting before burning for women.

Queen Chileshe's personal attendant, Nonde Ng'uni, had puked when the queen caught the duo red-handed, in *flagrante delicto*.

The queen felt like something was tearing open her cheeks with a blade when she saw them kissing. She felt nothing but repugnance for what she considered to be "their incorrigibly, unforgivable behavior."

"Perfect," began Chief Makasa, "here is our plan."

The plan involved killing the emperor after her had returned from offering sacrifices at the shrine. Doctor Besa Mungole would poison him with poison that kills slowly.

Meanwhile, without disclosing her pregnancy to the emperor the queen would drug him into having sex with her. The emperor would then get very sick and die. His death would be blamed on *imipashi* getting angry with him for violating the non-heat sexual encounters for the seer within three weeks of having made sacrifices.

Queen Chileshe would disclose to the elders that the emperor overpowered her, and due to pregnancy, she could not resist. Kabwe would testify, too, that he heard the queen struggling.

For the time being, the queen would assume the position of regent to the young, uncrowned emperor, Sampa. This position would enable Chief Makasa to take a central role in the empire by taking on the queen as his third wife, while the queen was bringing the entire *Lubemba* under Christianity, respectively.

"But what would happen to me, I don't want to die?" Kabwe, the emperor's assistant, who traditionally was supposed to be buried together with a dead king, grieved.

"Don't worry. That custom is only applicable if the emperor dies from natural causes or is assassinated or dies in war," Chief Makasa elucidated.

"And what about me?" Doctor Mungole asked.

"I think, to keep the secret, not only of your affair but also of poisoning the emperor, you need to continue on as Chief Palace Physician, and I will ensure that it is done when I am as regent," Queen Chileshe assured.

The *plan* pleased all the four and they agreed to implement it.

***

So, they plan *to kill him slowly, these broods of vipers. I will make sure that they are exposed. I, Nonde Ng'uni, will make everyone pay who was involved in the* carnage.

None of the four plotters knew that Nonde was listening to their conversation. She had, inadvertently, stumbled upon their meeting when she went to report to the queen about the impending *Ukusefya Pang'wena* celebrations.

That year's celebrations were delegated to the queen's office.

As Nonde thought about all these, there was a knock on her door.

CHAPTER 21 | SLUSH AND BURN

"Let us pray, huh," invoked Father Brantoon, "so that His Holiness, our Father, Bishop Joseph-Marie-Stanislas Dupont, will, by the grace of God and the favor of our Immaculate Mother, Mary the Virgin, be able to convince Chief Makasa Mwilwa Mukuka wa Mipini, as he would have his late father, Senior Chief Makasa Chisanga before him.

It was the second visit Bishop Dupont and Father Depillat were paying to the young chief who had succeeded his disgraced and ingloriously killed father. To please his lover and wife of the late emperor, the late Queen Ruth Mutale, Chief Makasa Chisenga had met then Father Dupont at Stevenson Road and Mambwe Mwela.

Soon as the congregants ended praying for their Bishop and his entourage, one of the congregation members, Brother Job Kambole, approached Father Brantoon and expressed his fears.

"Father, are we going to move from Kayambi, is the Holy Father going to look for land at Ng'wena?"

"We should not be contented with our settlement here, my son. The Lord would have us enter into the heart of the fish as our text today in Jonah.1:17 reminded us."

"Father, I will continue to pray so that our Holy Father is granted access. Since you came here, I have learned a lot. You're God's gift to us our people."

Father Brantoon remembered how hard it was when they first went to proclaim the Gospel in these lands. Children walked almost naked and had no knowledge of truth. They followed after false gods and paid homage to evil spirits. He further remembered how God worked a mighty miracle and confirmed their mission in these lands.

"Son, it was God's will for us to come to these lands."

"How do you know, Father, though the answer is obvious?"

"At first, it wasn't, my son. Bishop Lechaptois of Karema had sent us to attempt to convince Emperor Chiti III to open up a mission inside his headquarters. Due to illness and lack of a contact person at the palace, we failed."

"If you had failed, how would you call it God's will?"

"My son, as we were returning to Karema, we decided to take time and hunt. Then Father Dupont struck two guinea fowls with one stone. The birds fell a few meters away in the bushes. Unknown to us, the birds fell on top of two assassins who were trailing us; they were going to kill Father Dupont."

Brother Job was so enthused with the story that he ran inside the tent of meeting and brought a stool for Father Brantoon.

"Sit here, Father. I want to hear it all."

"Sure, my son, I surely have some Lord's time to spare. As I was saying, Emperor Chiti III, who never trusted missionaries, had wanted to kill our Holy Father. But those two birds saved our lives and opened doors of missionary work."

"How was that?"

"The two assassins returned and reported to the emperor that the God of our Bishop had reprimanded them. That when they were just about to shoot their arrows, God reprieved them by birds' whip."

"What happened, Father?"

"The emperor commanded them not to lay a hand on us after a servant of God in the palace, the late Queen Ruth, interpreted the occurrence as God's message to the emperor to open *Lubemba* for missionary work."

"Is it the same queen who was burned on the stake with late Senior Chief Makasa?"

"Yes, my son, indeed, God works in mysterious ways. Like her Lord, she gave up hers to bring many children to the Father."

"How was that possible, wasn't she involved in…"

"Adultery? My son?"

"Yes, Father."

"That is the understanding of the lost. For us, she was a Godsent. She was one grain of wheat that was planted to birth many."

"What is wheat, Father?"

"You see the 'bread' we use in Eucharist?"

"You mean, when we eat the body of Jesus and drink his blood?"

"Yes, my son. That *thing* we eat is made from wheat."

"Oh-oh, now I understand. Queen Mutale was our local Jesus?"

"Some sort of that, my son."

"Father, I am sorry, I diverted you."

"No issue, my son. Anyway, when the two assassins returned to their villages, the spread news that our God was powerful. We just saw a flood village taking Bishop Dupont away to their village and they began to worship him."

"Really, is it allowed, I mean, to worship another person?"

"No, my son. Father Dupont used the opportunity to introduce them to the one they should worship, who, he said, he worshiped."

"Our Lord Jesus Christ, isn't it, Father?"

"Yes, my son. We came to learn that the village where we had been brought was called Mambwe Mwela, and the Lord of that chiefdom was no one other than Senior Chief Makasa Chisenga."

"I see. So, that's how God opened doors in Mambweland?"

"Basically, yes."

ABOUT THE AUTHOR

Best Selling Author, Charles Mwewa (LLB; BA Law; BA Ed; LLM), is a prolific researcher, poet, novelist, lawyer, law professor and Christian apologist and intercessor. Mwewa has written no less than 85 books and counting in every genre and has exhibited his works at prestigious expos like the Ottawa International Book Expo and is the winner of the Coppa Awards for his signature publication, *Zambia: Struggles of My People*.
Mwewa and his family live in the Canadian Capital City of Ottawa.

SELECTED BOOKS BY THIS AUTHOR

1. *ZAMBIA: Struggles of My People (First and Second Editions)*
2. *10 FINANCIAL & WEALTH ATTITUDES TO AVOID*
3. *10 STRATEGIES TO DEFEAT STRESS AND DEPRESSION: Creating an Internal Safeguard against Stress and Depression*
4. *100+ REASONS TO READ BOOKS*
5. *A CASE FOR AFRICA?S LIBERTY: The Synergistic Transformation of Africa and the West into First-World Partnerships*
6. *A PANDEMIC POETRY, COVID-19*
7. *ALLERGIC TO CORRUPTION: The Legacy of President Michael Sata of Zambia*
8. *BOOK ABOUT SOMETHING: On Ultimate Purpose*
9. *CAMPAIGN FOR AFRICA: A Provocative Crusade for the Economic and Humanitarian Decolonization of Africa*
10. *CHAMPIONS: Application of Common Sense and Biblical Motifs to Succeed in Both Worlds*
11. *CORONAVIRUS PRAYERS*
12. *HH IS THE RIGHT MAN FOR ZAMBIA: And Other Acclaimed Articles on Zambia and Africa*
13. *I BOW: 3500 Prayer Lines of Inspiration & Intercession from the Heart: Volume One*
14. *INTERUNIVERSALISM IN A NUTSHELL: For Iranian Refugee Claimants*
15. *LAW & GRACE: An Expository Study in the Rudiments of Sin and Truth*
16. *LAWS OF INFLUENCE: 7even Lessons in Transformational Leadership*

www.ingramcontent.com/pod-product-compliance
Lightning Source LLC
Chambersburg PA
CBHW051821090426
42736CB00011B/1592